Curtis Cooks with Heart & Soul

Also by Curtis G. Aikens

Curtis Aikens' Guide to the Harvest

Curtis Cooks with

Heart & Soul

~~~

Curtis G. Aikens

Hearst Books
New York

It is the policy of William Morrow and Company, Inc., and its imprints and affiliates, recognizing the importance of preserving what has been written, to print the books we publish on acid-free paper, and we exert our best efforts to that end.

Library of Congress Cataloging-in-Publication Data

Aikens, Curtis.
      Curtis cooks with heart and soul /
Curtis G. Aikens; illustrations by Sara Mara Sturman
            p.   cm.
      Includes index.
      ISBN 0-688-14012-2
      1. Cookery, American—California style.   2. Vegetarian cookery.
I. Title.
TX715.2.C34A44 1995
641.59794—dc20   95-15122
                                                              CIP

Printed in the United States of America

    4 5 6 7 8 9 10

BOOK DESIGN BY RENATO STANISIC

This book is dedicated to my earthly lights:
my boys—Curtis George Aikens, Jr., and Cole Bennett Aikens.
I love you boys with everything I've got. My hope and prayer is
that someday our family will be whole.
This dedication extends to parents and children
everywhere who find themselves struggling to
stay a family despite divorce or separation.
May the God I love walk with you and keep you safe.

Acknowledgments

I can do all things through Christ who strengthens me. I thank the Lord for giving me the strength (all the strength) that helped me come through twenty-six years of not being able to read. Now, since I've learned, I've been able to pen another book.

As always, I acknowledge my parents, Eddie and Laura Aikens—I hope this makes you proud.

I want to thank my mother for being my teacher, for spending hours with me in the kitchen on this project and many others, and allowing me to stop her to measure the ingredients that she was using.

Alan Reid and Madi Land for believing in me and giving me work after the *Home Show* ended. You're not "like family" to me. You are family.

Bill Adler, my literary agent, for what you saw in me and liked. You're a special fellow, Bill.

My family: Mom and Dad; my brothers, Eddie and Jeffery; and my sisters, Laura Regina, Sophia, and Portia, for giving love and support.

Also to my California family: Keith Stafford; Vince and Sue Lattanzio; Mabel and Laura Turrini; my lawyer, Charles B. Tunnell; and Dr. Sophia Otis. I love you all so very much.

Jeni Hartman and Steve Seybold for teaching me to read. I have a lifetime of love for you.

To the Marin County Free Library, Literacy Volunteers of America (LVA) for being there, not only to teach me to read, but for teaching any adult.

Leonora Mays for Sharing Hawaii—the Aloha Spirit, Kona Coffee, great hugs, plenty of love, and garage sales (classic cookbooks).

Special thank-yous to Jean Potter and Eileen Wischusen for helping get this manuscript ready for the editors in New York, and to my TV Food Network family, may God bless all the meals we show America.

Finally, to Megan Newman and Jennifer Williams, my editors at Morrow. It's a pleasure working with you. Let's do it again!

Teresa and Catherine, may God bless.

Contents

Introduction

I grew up in a little town called Conyers, Georgia, about twenty-two miles east of Atlanta. My mom is and probably always will be the best cook, chef, and culinary guru I've ever known. Laura Bell (that's Mama's name) cooks wonderful, traditional Southern foods—soul food, if you will. When I was growing up, she cooked collard greens, black-eyed peas, corn bread, fried chicken, and green beans the traditional Southern way, using animal fat. And, boy, did I love it!

When I started to cook, I cooked the way my mom still does, and she cooks the way her teacher (Grandma) did, and she cooked the way her mother did, and so on down the line. I got really good at it. And got pretty big because of it, too. Back in the days when Grandma learned to cook, most African Americans worked in the fields all day, and burned off all that high-calorie and high-fat food. Nowadays we can't metabolize it the same way. In the early eighties, I decided to give up eating red meat in an attempt to lose weight, but I found out it's not just the intake of red meat that keeps weight on. I didn't lose very much weight until I started to exercise. However, I did discover that I don't have to have steak or ribs with every dinner, or bacon or sausage with every breakfast. This intrigued and inspired me to learn more about meatless meals.

I am not anti-meat or anti-poultry. The only thing that I am against is hatred. In fact, every day, on my television show (and I hope you've seen it on the TV Food Network), I stop before the last recipe to give a hug. I strongly believe in the theory that eight hugs a day keeps us going, and if you get more than eight, that's great.

Back to meatless meals. After giving up red meat, I found I didn't miss it. Well, that's not totally true. The one thing I craved was hamburger, and I don't think it was because of the taste. What I missed was the tradition, or the ease, of this habit, being able to order it at fast-food joints. During the early eighties I didn't know it was possible to order a veggie sandwich. Nowadays, I go into any fast-food restaurant and order a meatless veggie version of their popular burger. Feel free to do this yourself! Back when I began eating less red meat, all those wonderful grilled chicken and salad dishes that you can order these days weren't available at drive-through restaurants. Fortunately, I was living in California at the time, and that's where I first started seeing ground turkey in the local markets. In no time at all I was making turkey burgers.

A decade later, after I'd written my first book and signed a contract with ABC-TV (to become a regular cast member of the *Home Show*, where I gave tips on buying, using, storing, and cooking produce), I decided that if I wanted to be the best produce man ever, vegetables should be the focal point of my eating. So I decided to stop eating all meat: no chicken, no fish, no shellfish, no turkey, etc. I like to say that my motivation was—and still is—a quest for knowledge. I truly believe that the best way to write about something is to live it. If you want to write about vegetarian cooking, you should be vegetarian. Of course, there are many categories of vegetarian. At this point, I'm not vegan or macrobiotic, but who knows, in my quest for knowledge, I may eventually become one or the other. And I've got to tell you, the philosophy of writing about what you know best really does work! Since becoming a vegetarian I have created literally hundreds of recipes that are fun, easy to make, healthy, hearty, and great-tasting. In *Curtis Cooks with Heart and Soul,* I have integrated the two predominant influences on my cooking: California's light, fresh approach to cooking, and "soul," which, in one word for me, is Mama, and all the flavor and love she brought to the table. I have simply removed the meat and animal fat from the traditional dishes she taught me. I feel very confident that you're going to enjoy my renditions of those Southern favorites, as well as a few not-so-traditional dishes.

Curtis Cooks with Heart & Soul

Breads

I love bread, from the fancy focaccias I've found in Italian bistros, to the wonderful baguettes I've enjoyed on visits to Paris, to the hot bagels I've eaten in so many shops in New York City. I even love plain old store-bought loaf bread. As much as I enjoy these breads, though, none can compare to the breads from Mama's kitchen . . . the breads of my soul, the breads of my childhood in Mama's house in Conyers, Georgia. I hope the love I feel for the following recipes, as well as for the preparer, will come out at your table when you prepare them at home.

Mama's Corn Bread

Now, I can't tell you which of Mama's breads is my favorite, but suffice it to say, I love whatever I happen to be eating at the time. I'm starting this chapter with corn bread because it's the first bread I learned to make, and now that I do it well, I've created several recipes of my own from Mama's original. You are going to love this bread, particularly if you bake it like Mama and I do . . . in a large cast-iron skillet.

2 cups cornmeal

1 cup buttermilk

1 cup water

1 large egg

6 tablespoons
  vegetable oil

SERVES 4 TO 6

Preheat the oven to 375°F. In a mixing bowl, combine all the ingredients and mix well. On the stove top, heat the oil in a large skillet until hot but not boiling. Pour the hot oil into the bowl with the other ingredients and mix well. Pour the batter into the skillet and bake for 35 to 50 minutes. Start checking for doneness after 35 minutes; it should be golden brown when done.

Hush Puppies

3 cups vegetable oil, for deep frying (less than $1/2$ cup oil is absorbed by the hush puppies)

1 cup cornmeal

$1/2$ cup all-purpose flour

1 teaspoon cayenne pepper (whether it's labeled cayenne or red pepper in your part of the country, Mama says this is what makes these hush puppies great)

1 tablespoon sugar

1 small-to-medium onion, finely diced

1 cup buttermilk

1 large egg

$1/2$ cup water

When I was a kid, Friday was always fish day. Boy, can Mama cook fish! But as much as I looked forward to Friday, it wasn't the fish I was craving, it was those little, round, fried balls of onion and spice-filled batter we Southerners call hush puppies. Until you get the feel for making them, take your time. Like anything, the more you do it, the easier it gets. You're bound to love these as much as I do.

MAKES 1 DOZEN OR SO HUSH PUPPIES

Heat the oil to 350°F in a large pot or deep fryer. Combine all the ingredients except the water in a bowl. If the batter is too stiff to slide from a tablespoon into the oil, add as much of the water, a little at a time, as is needed to soften it. Drop the batter into the hot oil, a tablespoonful at a time. The batter will sink to the bottom of the pot, then float to the top when done. I always roll the hush puppies around for a few seconds longer to make sure their centers are cooked through.

Mama's No-Name Bread

When I was growing up, this bread never had a name. It's one Mama just whipped up in no time. Fried as patties in much the same way you would make pancakes, this bread is delicious with soups.

MAKES UP TO 1 ½ DOZEN PATTIES

In a mixing bowl, combine all the ingredients except the oil. In a frying pan, heat about half of the oil to 350°F. Using a large soup spoon or ladle, put the batter in the hot oil and fry until done, about 1 to 2 minutes on each side. Add more of the oil as needed.

2 cups cornmeal

1 cup buttermilk

1 cup water

1 large egg

1 cup vegetable oil, for frying

Biscuits of Love

3 cups all-purpose flour

¹/₂ cup shortening (Mama says, "Nothing but Crisco.")

³/₄ cup buttermilk

¹/₂ cup water

One of my life's beautiful experiences is watching my mother make biscuits. Her fingers work the dough as though she were signing a special message. I've always thought she might be subconsciously spelling the word "Love" in each biscuit. One day I'll take a series of pictures of Mama making her biscuits. I'll call them "Making Love."

MAKES 12 NICE BISCUITS

Preheat the oven to 400°F and grease a baking sheet. Mix the flour and shortening together in a bowl, combining them well with your fingers. Slowly add the buttermilk and water until the dough is firm. Form the dough into 12 biscuits, place them on the baking sheet, and bake them for 10 to 15 minutes.

Garlic and Onion Corn Bread

When I was growing up in Georgia, there was no shortage of fresh food. Granddaddy Curtis was a great farmer, and Dad was pretty good when he wanted to be. But in California, I was introduced to garden foods that Granddaddy and Dad would have never thought to plant.

On my first cross-country trip to California, my road warrior buddy, Bill Hope, and I spent a great week in San Diego, where I had my first taste of an avocado. Though that was a wonderful experience, the best was yet to come. Traveling north, to get to the coast, we took Route 152 west which directed us through Gilroy. It was late at night, and moonless, so we could see only what was in the path of the car's headlights. But, oh, could we smell. The aroma of garlic filled the air, and I remember saying to Bill that there must be a spaghetti factory nearby. Hey, back in the early eighties, I didn't know that Gilroy was considered the *garlic capital*.

The memory of that trip helped create this savory bread, and I hope you love it as much as I do.

1 recipe Mama's Corn Bread (page 3)

1 bulb garlic, chopped not minced (Yes, you heard me right. A bulb is the entire head of the garlic, not an individual clove. This recipe is really garlicky, and if you're like me, 2 bulbs isn't too much.)

1 small-to-medium onion, chopped

Bunch of green onions, chopped

SERVES 4 TO 6

Preheat the oven to 375°F. In a mixing bowl, combine all the ingredients except the oil and mix well. On the stove top, heat the oil in a large skillet until hot but not boiling. Pour the hot oil into the bowl with the other ingredients and mix well. Pour the batter into the skillet and bake for 35 minutes, or until done. Start checking for doneness after 35 minutes; it should be golden brown when done.

Herbs

In California, I found many herbs I had never heard of, much less tasted: chervil, tarragon, coriander, cilantro, rosemary, sage, and thyme. These days, fresh and dried herbs are such a large part of my cooking that I have to really think hard to remember the days of just salt and pepper. The following recipes use some of those wonderful flavors.

Herb Corn Bread

Remember, I love a strong herb flavoring, so if this recipe seems heavy on the herbs to you, start with half the suggested amounts. The first time I prepared this bread, I used fresh thyme, oregano, basil, and sage . . . about two tablespoons of each. In the years since, I've used many, many combinations. Don't feel stuck with my choice of herbs. Be adventurous and try your own combinations. If the herbs are dried, use only one and a half teaspoons of each, and add them either to the batter or to the buttermilk. Just remember to increase the buttermilk by two to three tablespoons when using dried herbs. This is another recipe that builds on Mama's basic corn bread, and it is wonderful. I love to crumble it into soups and use it in stuffings.

1 recipe Mama's Corn Bread (page 3)

2 tablespoons each fresh thyme, oregano, basil, and sage, or 1$^1/_2$ teaspoons each dried thyme, oregano, basil, and sage

2 to 3 tablespoons buttermilk

SERVES 4 TO 6

Preheat the oven to 375°F. In a mixing bowl, combine all the ingredients except the oil and mix well. On the stove top, heat the oil in a large skillet until hot but not boiling. Pour the hot oil into the bowl with the other ingredients and mix well. Pour the batter into the skillet and bake for 35 to 50 minutes. Start checking for doneness after 35 minutes; it should be golden brown when done.

Sweet and Hot Corn Bread

SWEET CORN BREAD

1 recipe Mama's Corn Bread (page 3)

1 teaspoon ground cinnamon

1 teaspoon ground nutmeg

1/2 teaspoon ground ginger

1/2 teaspoon ground cloves

1 to 2 tablespoons sugar (If you add another 2 to 3 tablespoons of sugar, the bread becomes more like dessert.)

1 teaspoon vanilla extract or almond extract

HOT CORN BREAD

1 recipe Mama's Corn Bread (page 3)

1/2 teaspoon ground mustard seed

1/2 teaspoon freshly ground black and/or white peppercorns

1/2 teaspoon chili powder

Dash of cumin

There are two sides to spices: sweet and hot. I enjoy both. The hot corn bread is especially good with meatless chili.

SERVES 4 TO 6

Preheat the oven to 375°F. In a mixing bowl, combine all the ingredients except the oil and mix well. On the stove top, heat the oil in a large skillet until hot but not boiling. Pour the hot oil into the bowl with the other ingredients and mix well. Pour the batter into the skillet and bake for 35 to 50 minutes. Start checking for doneness after 35 minutes; it should be golden brown when done.

Basic Pizza Dough

~~~

Like Mama's corn bread, my pizza dough recipe is a good base for many variations. Make a batch or two of this pizza dough recipe, and try the recipes that follow it. Then enjoy experimenting on your own.

MAKES ONE 10- TO 12-INCH CRUST

1 package yeast

$^1/_2$ teaspoon sugar

$^3/_4$ cup warm water

2 cups all-purpose flour

Dash of salt

2 tablespoons olive oil or other vegetable oil

Mix the yeast, sugar, and water in a small bowl. Proof the yeast by letting it stand 5 to 10 minutes until bubbles form. Sift the flour and salt into a large mixing bowl. Add the oil and yeast mixture to the dry ingredients. With a wooden spoon, mix thoroughly until the dough is smooth, or use the world's best mixer, your hands. After the dough forms, continue kneading and working it until all the flour is incorporated and the texture is smooth. Let the dough rest in an oiled mixing bowl for 20 to 30 minutes. Then punch it down and roll it out to make a pizza or another recipe using it.

Garlic Knots

~~~

1/2 recipe Basic Pizza Dough
(page 11)

2 garlic cloves, chopped

1/2 cup extra virgin
olive oil

The inspiration for this recipe came from New York City. After spending an incredible day with my agent and editor, I was headed for the airport and I mentioned to the cab driver that I hadn't had a chance to get a slice of New York pizza. That's one of my rituals when I'm in the city. Next thing I knew, he was double-parked outside a place on Fifty-fifth or Fifty-seventh Street. Behind the counter were obviously a pop-and-son duo. With that great New York accent, the younger one said, "What uh ya have?" As my slice was heating, I caught a glimpse of some beautiful, oily garlic-covered knots. The older man must have seen the curious look on my face and offered me one. And I ended up buying a dozen. Here's my version of their garlic knots.

MAKES ABOUT 18 KNOTS

Make 1 recipe of pizza dough. After it rises, separate it into 2 pieces, setting aside 1 piece to use for focaccia or another recipe.

Preheat the oven to 375° to 400°F. Divide the dough into as many golf-ball-sized pieces as you can make. Roll each out to a 4- to 6-inch-long piece, then loop it into a pretzel-shaped knot, pushing the dough together. Add the chopped garlic to the olive oil. You can then either roll the knots in the garlic and oil and bake them for 8 to 10 minutes until they are golden brown, making wonderful toasted garlic knots, or you can bake the knots first, then roll them in the garlic and oil.

Focaccia

~~~~~~

So what do you do with the other half of that pizza dough? Make focaccia. Focaccia is basically cooked pizza bread, which can have a sauce on it or just vegetables on it. When I lived in New York City for a couple of years in the late eighties, I had some wonderful, food-related jobs. One place I worked was Balducci's, the gourmet market on Sixth Avenue in the Village. One thing I really loved was sampling the many focaccias in the store. Next time you have a chance to travel to New York, stop by Balducci's and do some sampling. Also, head a little farther south to Dean & Deluca and the Gourmet Garage in SoHo and try their focaccia. There's plenty more uptown, too, at Zabar's on the west side and at the Gourmet Garage's relative on the east side. Try everybody's focaccia! Then try mine.

1 small-to-medium onion, chopped

1 small-to-medium ripe tomato, diced

$1/2$ recipe Basic Pizza Dough (the unused half from the Garlic Knots) (page 11)

$1/4$ teaspoon assorted herbs such as rosemary, basil, and oregano (optional)

$1/4$ stick (1 ounce) butter, melted, or olive oil

SERVES 4 TO 6

Preheat the oven to 400°F. Work the onion and tomato into the pizza dough. If you want to get fancy, you can add some herbs along with the onion and tomato. Roll the dough out as flat as you like. (I roll mine out to about 6 to 7 inches for a thicker bread.) Bake on an oiled baking sheet for about 15 minutes, or until golden brown. Just before removing the focaccia from the oven, brush the top with melted butter.

Cinnamon Things

1 recipe Basic Pizza Dough
  (page 11)

$^1/_2$ stick (2 ounces) butter

2 tablespoons ground
  cinnamon

$^1/_2$ cup sugar plus an
  additional $^1/_4$ to $^1/_2$ cup
  to sweeten the dough
  (optional)

As much as I love sweets, store-bought cinnamon rolls covered in confectioners' icing are just too sugary for me in the morning. My Cinnamon Things aren't like that. Not only are they great in the morning, they're wonderful anytime of the day. If your sweet tooth is sweeter than mine, work a quarter to a half a cup of sugar into the dough before rolling it out.

SERVES 4 TO 6

Make the pizza dough. Preheat the oven to 375° to 400°F. Divide the dough in half. Roll each half out flat, either into a circle or a square. Spread the butter over the top of each half. Mix the cinnamon and sugar together and sprinkle over the butter. Roll each half into a log. Cut the logs into slices about 1 inch thick and bake them for approximately 12 minutes.

Easy Loaf Bread

This is a heavy bread, and I love it. I always slice it right out of the oven, though the bread does seem to slice better after it has cooled down a little.

1 recipe Basic Pizza Dough (page 11)

MAKES 2 LOAVES

Make the pizza dough, then let it sit in a oiled bowl for 2, 3, or even 4 hours. Make sure the bowl is in a warm spot. Grease 2 loaf pans with vegetable oil.

Divide the dough into 2 equal pieces, then place them in the prepared loaf pans. Preheat the oven to 400°F while the dough rests in the pans for 5 to 10 minutes. Bake for about 45 minutes. (I start checking for doneness after about 30 minutes.) If you want to keep the top from getting too crusty, place a tin foil tent over the dough during the first 25 minutes of baking.

Maize Cakes

1/4 cup canola oil, for frying, plus more if needed

1 pound potatoes, baked and mashed

2 cups masa harina

1 teaspoon baking powder

1 cup fresh corn kernels

1 cup grated sharp cheese

2 tablespoons Tomato Salsa (page 169)

Salt and freshly ground black pepper to taste

2 tablespoons water, plus more if needed

I've created this recipe in tribute to the times I spend in the Navajo Nation. In 1993 when a "mystery ailment" struck the Navajo Nation, just by chance I was there, visiting a friend and sharing with the Navajo kids my love of reading. I was invited to a tribal meeting and was informed after the meeting that no outsiders are ever allowed in that conclave. It was a great honor for me to be allowed in, and an even greater honor to break bread with the Navajo elders. One of the dishes we ate was maize cakes, which reminded me very much of my mother's corn fritters. This also reinforces my belief that many of our cultural problems, in this country and around the world, can be solved when we start "breaking bread" together. We can see how much we have in common, including our foods. Those semisweet corn cakes were wonderful, and I hope my friends among the Navajos enjoy my version of their home dish.

MAKES UP TO 3 DOZEN PATTIES

In a large frying pan, heat the oil to 375°F. Mix together the potatoes, masa harina, baking powder, corn, cheese, salsa, salt and pepper, and water. Form the mixture into patties and fry, turning them once, until they are golden brown, about 6 minutes. You can serve them hot or cold; I think they're better hot.

Soups, Chowders, Chilis, and Stews

Soups *When I think of soup, I think of my parents... my mama,*

because of the great ritual involved in the preparation of her soups, and my dad,

because soup was absolutely the only food he would accept as a one-dish meal.

Mind you, he did have to have corn bread or crackers, but he didn't require a salad

or side dish or even a dessert, for that matter. That's because Mama's soups and

stews were, and still are, several courses in a single pot. From start to finish,

Mama's soups could contain as many as twenty different ingredients.

Mama would be the first to tell you that the secret to good soup is the foundation,

or base ... the stock. She would start with the meat or bones, brown them a bit

with some seasoning and maybe some herbs and onions. She'd then add water and

let the base simmer an hour or so before adding the root vegetables. All of that

cooked together for another hour or more, then she would add the next batch of

vegetables. When we kids got home from school, the house was full of the most

wonderful, warm smell, and by the time Dad came in from work, the house smelled great! She'd make up a big skillet of corn bread, and what a meal it would be! Dad's right. You don't need to serve anything more when you have a pot of homemade soup on the table.

That's how I remember soup as a kid. Now that I'm an adult, I've discovered something else about soup. Picture this: It's a cold, late night. You're in the Village in New York, or North Beach in San Francisco, or a favorite spot you share with a special person. The two of you step into a quaint café, sit by the window, and, shivering from the chill of the night, order a big bowl of steaming, hot soup. One bowl, two spoons. Each time the spoons go into the bowl, your heads lower and your eyes meet. Who would have thought soup could be romantic. Wonder if Dad knew? Let's make some soup!

Three Recipes for Vegetable Stock

Back when I lived in Mama's house, I dare say 99 percent of her soups were meat-based, and they would cook all day, or so it seemed. My soups are totally meatless, made from a vegetable stock, and they taste great. I've included three vegetable stocks here: Super Stock (page 21), Thick Stock (page 22), and Quick Stock (page 23). When one is called for, you should use the one of your choice. Lots of people think meatless soups have a tendency to be watery, and personally, I hate nothing more than a thin, watery bowl of vegetarian soup. But if you remember Mama's words, "Remember the base, the stock," I promise you'll never worry about thin, watery soups again.

Super Stock

This is my all-purpose stock, which is great for cooking rice or pasta, or when it's added to stuffing. It is also very easy to make and takes about forty minutes from start to finish. I peel the carrots and parsnip, which makes the soup stock stronger. It is as if the flavor pours out from the vegetables when the skin is removed.

MAKES ABOUT 3 CUPS

Put the water, carrots, parsnip, celery, and onion in a stock-pot and bring to a boil. Stir in the butter, salt, and pepper and lower the heat to medium. Cover and simmer for 40 minutes. Remove the pot from the heat and strain the stock through a sieve. This stock can be stored in the refrigerator until you're ready to use it, or it can be frozen.

2 cups water

2 carrots, peeled and cut into 1-inch pieces

1 parsnip, peeled and cut into 1-inch pieces

6 celery stalks, cut into 1-inch pieces

$^1/_2$ large onion, quartered, or 1 whole medium onion

$^1/_4$ stick (1 ounce) butter or margarine or 2 table-spoons vegetable oil

1 teaspoon salt

$^1/_2$ teaspoon freshly ground black pepper

Thick Stock

2 cups water

2 carrots, peeled and cut into 1-inch pieces

1 parsnip, peeled and cut into 1-inch pieces

6 celery stalks, cut into 1-inch pieces

1 yellow squash, cut into 1-inch pieces

$^1/_4$ stick (1 ounce) butter or margarine or 2 table-spoons vegetable oil

$^1/_2$ teaspoon salt

$^1/_2$ teaspoon freshly ground black pepper

I use this stock for thicker soups and soup-based sauces. It takes a bit longer than Super Stock and is somewhat milder because of the absence of the onion.

MAKES ABOUT 3 CUPS

Put the water, carrots, parsnip, and celery in a stockpot and bring to a boil. Add the remaining ingredients, lower the heat, and simmer, covered, for about 1 hour. Taste and adjust the seasonings if necessary. Remove the pot from the heat and discard all but about $^1/_2$ cup of the vegetables. With a hand-held mixer, or in a food processor or blender, purée the remaining vegetables in the broth to make the broth thick. (For an even thicker broth, leave more of the vegetables.)

Quick Stock

When I'm short on time and really want homemade soup, I make this stock. You can have a wonderful vegetable soup in thirty minutes or less with this recipe.

MAKES 1 TO 2 CUPS

2 bunches of celery, stalks separated and washed

1 tablespoon butter

Salt and freshly ground black pepper to taste

Run the celery stalks through a juicer if you have one, or chop them and purée them in a food processor or blender. Strain the purée and discard the pulp. In a saucepan, heat the juice with the butter, salt, and pepper over medium heat until heated through. You now have the base for a wonderful soup.

Three Mushroom Soup

2 to 3 tablespoons olive oil

10 medium white or brown
mushrooms, washed and
thinly sliced

4 ounces oyster mushrooms,
washed and thinly sliced

2 ounces shiitake mushrooms,
washed and thinly sliced

1 medium onion, diced

2 cups vegetable stock
(page 20)

1 tablespoon Worcestershire
sauce

Salt and freshly ground black
pepper to taste

This soup is excellent, but to make it really special, purée the sautéed mushrooms and onion with a hand-held mixer or in a food processor or blender before adding them to the stock.

SERVES 2 TO 4

In a large stockpot, heat the oil. Add the mushrooms and onion, cover, and sauté over medium heat for 7 to 10 minutes, stirring occasionally. Add the vegetable stock and bring to a boil. Lower the heat to medium and add the Worcestershire sauce and salt and pepper. Cook for about 30 minutes. Before serving, adjust the seasoning if necessary.

Creamy Mushroom Soup

With this, or any recipe that calls for mushrooms, feel free to be creative. Mix and match them. Use everything from wild mushrooms to button mushrooms to dried mushrooms. Have fun.

SERVES 3 TO 4

In a large pot, sauté the mushrooms, shallots, and garlic in the butter till the shallots are translucent, about 4 minutes. Then clear a spot in the middle of the pot, add the flour and stir to make a paste, then add a bit of the stock to form a roux. Add the remainder of the stock, the half-and-half, and the nutmeg. Season with salt and pepper. Bring to a boil, lower the heat and simmer about 25 minutes. Then in a food processor or blender, purée the soup until smooth. Serve it immediately, garnished with the parsley and dill.

1 pound mushrooms, sliced

2 shallots, chopped

2 garlic cloves, crushed

$1/2$ stick (2 ounces) butter

3 tablespoons all-purpose flour

2 cups vegetable stock (page 20)

2 cups half-and-half

Pinch of freshly ground nutmeg

Salt and freshly ground black pepper to taste

$1/4$ cup minced fresh parsley, for garnish

Fresh dill, for garnish

Roasted Red Pepper and Tomato Soup

2 large red bell peppers, roasted, peeled, seeded, and cut into bits

2 large tomatoes, peeled and diced

4 garlic cloves, chopped

1 teaspoon dried oregano

1 cup vegetable stock (page 20)

$1/2$ tablespoon Worcestershire sauce

$1/4$ cup heavy cream

2 teaspoons sugar

My lawyer, Charles B. Tunnell, and I were having our annual Christmas lunch at the Savannah Grill in Corte Madera, California. We both ordered soup . . . two bowls, two spoons . . . and with our first taste began the great adventure of trying to identify the ingredients. We could taste garlic and oregano, and the red peppers, tomato, and cream. But there was something else. After repeated testing and tasting, I discovered the something else is Worcestershire sauce.

SERVES 2 TO 3

Place the peppers, tomatoes, garlic, and oregano in a medium pot along with the stock. Cover and bring to a boil. Cook for 10 minutes, then reduce the heat to simmer. Add the Worcestershire sauce and simmer an additional hour and 10 minutes, covered. Remove from the heat and add the cream and sugar. Then using a hand-held mixer, or in a blender or food processor, purée the soup until smooth. Serve immediately.

Note: To roast peppers, brush the peppers with olive oil and put them in a roasting pan. Place them under the broiler until their skins swell and blacken. Turn the peppers several times to roast on all sides.

You can store roasted peppers in the refrigerator for up to 2 weeks. I recommend storing them for at least several days to bring out more of the sweetness of the peppers which isn't there straight out of the oven. A flavorful juice is also extracted from the peppers during refrigeration.

Pumpkin Soup

Here's another restaurant-inspired soup, this time from New York. This is about the best soup I've ever tasted in a restaurant, and since I can't seem to remember the name or exact location of the restaurant, I've created my own recipe. I had this wonderful soup around Halloween when pumpkins are plentiful, but when I went to the market in search of pumpkins, they were out. So, I just substituted butternut squash. Even in pies, butternut squash is a great substitute for pumpkin. In fact, when I made this soup with butternut squash, it tasted exactly like the soup from the restaurant, which leads me to believe they, too, may have used butternut squash.

SERVES 2 TO 4

In a large pot, sauté the pumpkin in the oil and butter, covered, for about 10 minutes. Add the onion, celery, and stock and cook an additional 10 minutes. Add the water and potato. Combine the ingredients well, then add the Worcestershire sauce and salt and pepper. Cook until the potatoes are soft, about 20 to 30 minutes. (At the restaurant, the soup was puréed, but I choose not to do that with my recipe, which results in a more homemade-textured soup.)

3/4 pound pumpkin or butternut squash, cut into 1-inch cubes

2 tablespoons olive oil

1/4 stick (1 ounce) butter

1 medium onion, diced

2 celery stalks, diced

1 cup vegetable stock (page 20)

1/2 cup water

1 medium potato, peeled and cut into large dice

1 tablespoon Worcestershire sauce

Salt and freshly ground black pepper to taste

Pumpkin-Tomato Delight

1 onion, chopped

½ stick (2 ounces) butter

1 28-ounce can tomatoes

1 tablespoon dark brown
  sugar

4 cups pumpkin purée

4 cups vegetable stock
  (page 20)

This is one of those recipes I just fell upon. It is the result of a refrigerator full of leftovers and not much else. The combination of pumpkin, tomatoes, and onions makes for a great soup. And if you have other leftovers, feel free to throw them in. This soup, I feel, will be the next generation's "comfort food."

SERVES 4 TO 6

In a large pot, sauté the onion in the butter until the onion is translucent. Add the tomatoes, sugar, pumpkin purée, and stock. Heat through for about 20 to 30 minutes.

Tomato Soup

Tomatoes are one of America's most popular produce items in both consumption and sales. Mama has always said, "If you've got a good tomato soup, you've got the makings for a great meal in one pot." Add a couple of potatoes and you've got tomato-potato soup. Add cream and you've got cream of tomato soup.

Is the tomato a fruit or a vegetable?

SERVES 2 TO 3

In a medium pot, heat the olive oil and butter and sauté the onion, parsnip, and carrot about 3 minutes. Add the tomatoes and cook, covered, about 5 minutes. Pour in the stock and bring to a boil. Lower the heat and simmer about 30 minutes. Season with salt and pepper. In a food processor or blender, purée the soup until smooth and serve it immediately. (If the soup is too strong, add ¼ cup of water to weaken it.)

(By the way, a tomato is botanically a fruit. Back in the late 1800s, however, the Supreme Court declared it a vegetable due to certain tariffs.)

3 tablespoons olive oil

1 tablespoon butter

1 onion, diced

¹/₂ parsnip, peeled and diced

1 carrot, peeled and diced

2 large tomatoes, peeled and diced

1 cup vegetable stock (page 20)

¹/₂ teaspoon salt

¹/₄ teaspoon freshly ground black pepper

Vegetable, Tomato, and Rice Soup

1 cup shredded cabbage

2 carrots, peeled and diced

1 zucchini, diced

1 yellow squash, diced

3 cups water

Bunch of broccoli, stems removed, cut into big florets

3 medium cauliflower florets, quartered

1¹/₂ cups vegetable stock (page 20)

5 tablespoons (2¹/₂ ounces) butter

¹/₂ cup long grain rice

1 large tomato, peeled and diced

1 large onion, diced

Salt and freshly ground black pepper to taste

On cold, wintry days, I like to make this thick and hearty soup and fill my house with its wonderful aroma. My house is in the woods way out in the country, and I like nothing more than to fix myself a bowl of vegetable, tomato, and rice soup and sit by the window, looking at the wildlife in my woods. This is a true comfort dish. It makes me imagine the world at peace.

SERVES 2 TO 4

Put the cabbage, carrots, zucchini, and yellow squash in a large stockpot. Pour in ¹/₂ cup of the water and cook over high heat about 10 minutes. Add the broccoli, cauliflower, stock, 3 tablespoons of the butter, and another ¹/₂ cup of the water. Bring to a boil and cook 15 minutes. Add the remaining 2 cups of water and return to a boil. Stir in the rice, tomato, and onion. Reduce the heat and simmer until the rice is done, about 20 to 30 minutes. Stir in the remaining 2 tablespoons of butter and season with salt and pepper.

Tomato and Potato Soup

You can actually make several versions of this soup. Try it substituting one half to three quarters of a cup of rice for the potatoes. The result is a thicker soup, and one that tastes great. You might also try pasta instead of the potatoes. You can either precook the pasta, which allows the soup to remain thin, or cook the pasta in the soup, creating a thicker texture. It's wonderful either way.

SERVES 2 TO 4

Put the oils and butter in a large pot. Add the onions, celery, and carrot and sauté for about 3 minutes. Add the tomatoes. Cover and cook about 5 minutes. Add the stock and bring to a boil. Lower the heat and simmer about 30 minutes. Season with the salt and pepper and purée the mixture. (I use a hand-held blender and purée right in the pot, but you can also use a blender or food processor.) To the puréed mixture, add the water, potatoes, and garlic. Bring to a boil and cook 5 to 10 minutes, uncovered. Watch the soup closely and stir often to keep it from drying out and burning on the bottom. Lower the heat and add the basil and okra. Cover and simmer, stirring occasionally, until the okra softens and the soup thickens.

2 tablespoons vegetable oil

2 tablespoons olive oil

$1/4$ stick (1 ounce) butter

2 onions, diced

2 celery stalks, chopped

1 carrot, peeled and diced

2 large tomatoes, peeled and diced

1 cup vegetable stock (page 20)

$1/2$ teaspoon salt

$1/4$ teaspoon freshly ground black pepper

$1^1/2$ cups water

3 medium potatoes, peeled and cut into 1-inch chunks

3 whole garlic cloves, peeled

4 ounces fresh basil

5 medium okra, stems removed, cut into $1/4$- inch pieces

Leek, Potato, and Asparagus Soup

~~~~~~

2 tablespoons vegetable oil
or olive oil

1/4 stick (1 ounce) butter

2 large leeks, washed and
chopped (you can use the
green tops, but wash them
well since they can be
quite sandy)

1 celery stalk, chopped

1 large onion, chopped

2 large potatoes, peeled
and cut into 1-inch cubes

1 1/2 cups water

1/2 to 3/4 pound asparagus,
cut into 1/2-inch pieces,
with tips intact

2 cups milk

1/2 cup heavy cream

Salt and freshly ground
black pepper to taste

3 whole green onions,
chopped, for garnish

When I was a kid, I don't think my mama ever made potato leek soup, though she often made soups using potatoes and onions as the base ingredients. I remember Mama saying she would use potatoes and onions to thicken soups and for additional flavor. In fact, you can make a quick, easy broth simply by boiling a potato and onion together with one to two tablespoons of butter. It's quite starchy, but it's great for thick soups. Taking her idea a bit further, I've created a leek, potato, and asparagus soup. The leek, of course, is an onion and is used for flavor; the potato is for thickening; and the asparagus . . . well, just because I love it.

SERVES 3 TO 4

Put the oil, butter, leeks, celery, and onion in a large pot. Cover and cook about 8 minutes, stirring every minute or so, until the onion is translucent and the leeks have softened. Add the potatoes and water. Bring to a boil, lower the heat to medium, and cook until the potatoes are soft, about 12 to 15 minutes. Add the asparagus, milk, and cream. Stir and cook, covered, at least 5 minutes longer. Season with salt and pepper, and sprinkle the chopped green onions on top of the soup just before serving. Wonderful soup!

Artichoke Soup

Being a Southerner, I like to serve corn bread with many of my dishes because I really enjoy the contribution corn bread makes to a meal. Oftentimes, you can change the presentation and flavor of a meal simply by the bread you serve it with. Artichoke soup is so versatile that by serving it with the breads of your region, you've created a special meal unique to your own way of life. I particularly enjoy serving artichoke soup with French bread cut into thick slices, but if you're from San Francisco, you might try sourdough; or brown bread if you're from New England; or if you live in the heartland, maybe a flatbread. This is a great soup, just waiting for you to add your own special touch.

SERVES 6

Quarter the artichoke hearts and place them with the rest of the ingredients in a large stockpot. Bring to a boil. Cover and simmer on low heat for about 2 hours. For a thicker soup, remove the lid the last 20 minutes of cooking.

2 medium fresh artichoke hearts, cooked

1 parsnip, peeled and chopped

1 small yellow onion, chopped

3 celery stalks, chopped

1 small turnip, peeled and chopped

1 leek, washed and diced (you can use the green tops, but wash them well since they can be quite sandy)

$1/4$ cup chopped fresh parsley

2 tablespoons lemon juice

1 teaspoon butter

$1/2$ teaspoon ground coriander

6 cups vegetable stock (page 20)

$1/4$ cup dry white wine

Salt and freshly ground black pepper to taste

Vegetable Noodle Soup

3/4 cup water

2 carrots, peeled and sliced

2 celery stalks, chopped

1 zucchini, sliced

Bunch of broccoli, stems removed, cut into large florets

3 large cauliflower florets, cut into quarters

1 cup vegetable stock (page 20)

3 tablespoons (1 1/2 ounces) unsalted butter

6 ounces cooked pasta of your choice

Grated Parmesan cheese, to taste

Soup is good for using up leftovers. Throw in some pasta, a few stalks of celery and a carrot, and maybe a bit of broccoli. Add vegetable stock and the other ingredients, and you have an easy, tasty, healthy soup. I like the following combination, but feel free to improvise with whatever you have in the refrigerator.

SERVES 3 TO 4

Put 1/4 cup of the water in a large pot and add the carrots, celery, and zucchini. Steam until soft, about 10 minutes. Add the broccoli, cauliflower, stock, remaining 1/2 cup water, and 2 tablespoons of the butter. Bring to a boil and reduce the heat to medium. Cook about 15 to 20 minutes. Add the pasta and the remaining tablespoon of butter. Heat thoroughly and serve with grated Parmesan cheese.

Easy Lentil-Spinach Soup

This recipe is amazingly simple, yet the dish is filling and flavor-packed. I love the combination of lentil, spinach, and potatoes, along with the nutty, sweet flavor of squash. Once you try this soup on a cold winter day, it may become a weekly habit.

SERVES 3 TO 4

Place all the ingredients in a large pot and bring to a boil. Lower the heat to simmer and cook, covered, about 45 to 50 minutes. Remove the bay leaves before serving.

1 pound lentils

2 cups vegetable stock (page 20)

2 tablespoons coriander seeds

2 tablespoons cumin seeds

1 teaspoon dried oregano

1 teaspoon dried basil

2 bay leaves

3 or 4 small red potatoes, diced

1 pound fresh spinach, thoroughly rinsed and chopped

3 cups peeled and diced butternut squash

1 tablespoon olive oil

1 large onion, chopped

1 celery stalk, chopped

1 carrot, peeled and thinly sliced

4 garlic cloves, crushed

Salt and freshly ground black pepper to taste

Split Pea Soup

2 quarts water

2 cups split peas

2 bay leaves

3 tablespoons olive oil

Salt to taste

3 onions, minced

3 garlic cloves, minced

1 tablespoon ground cumin

2 celery stalks, diced

2 to 3 carrots, diced

1/4 stick (1 ounce) butter

When I make split pea soup, boy, do I make it! When I was a kid, Mama made split pea soup using ham. I've been able to take the pork out and still leave the punch in by using olive oil, minced onions, garlic, and cumin.

SERVES 4 TO 6

In a large pot, bring the water to a boil. Add the split peas, bay leaves, 1 tablespoon of the oil, and salt to the water. Cook for 20 to 30 minutes. In a saucepan, sauté the onions, garlic, and cumin in the remaining 2 tablespoons of the oil, until the onions are translucent, about 2 to 3 minutes. Add the onion mixture, celery, and carrots to the pot. Simmer, uncovered, for about 30 minutes. Remove the bay leaves, adjust the seasonings, and add the butter just before serving.

Onion Soup

If you want a guarantee that you won't cry while cutting onions, put on your sunglasses. Reason? The shades keep the onion vapors from reaching your eyes.

SERVES 4 TO 6

Heat the oil and butter in a saucepan and sauté the onions, covered, for 10 minutes, or until they are golden brown. Uncover the pan and increase the heat, adding the stock, thyme, and salt. Cover and let the soup simmer for about 30 minutes. Make a paste with the flour and water and add it to the soup. Simmer an additional 20 minutes and add the croutons and cheese just before serving.

1 tablespoon vegetable oil

$^1/_2$ stick (4 ounces) butter

2 large onions, thinly sliced

2 quarts vegetable stock (page 20)

1 teaspoon fresh thyme

1 teaspoon salt

$1^1/_2$ tablespoons all-purpose flour

2 tablespoons water

1 recipe Homemade Croutons (page 61)

2 cups grated Cheddar cheese

Egg Soup

2¹/₂ cups vegetable stock
(page 20)

¹/₄ cup celery leaves

Salt and freshly ground black
pepper to taste

1 large egg

Juice of 1 lemon

¹/₃ cup cooked long
grain rice

Talk about a quick and simple soup . . . this is one. I love to mix this with my Hot and Sour Soup (page 39) and a couple of tablespoons of sweet and sour sauce. This soup is thinner than most of my soups, but it delivers lots of flavor and nutrients.

SERVES 3 TO 4

In a medium saucepan, simmer the stock with the celery leaves for about 10 minutes. Remove the celery leaves and season the stock with salt and pepper. Beat the egg and lemon juice in a bowl to which ¼ cup of the stock has been added. Pour the egg mixture into the saucepan. Add the rice, adjust the seasoning, and serve.

Hot and Sour Soup

This is a classic in Chinese restaurants, and here's my version. The cider and soy sauce are the sour, and the cayenne pepper makes it hot. If it's too hot for your palate, add about a tablespoon of duck sauce to each serving.

SERVES 3 TO 4

In a medium pot, bring the stock to a boil and add the mushrooms, vinegar, soy sauce, and cayenne. In a small bowl, combine the cornstarch with the water and pour the paste into the stock. Add the bamboo, tofu, and egg and continue cooking until ingredients are tender and mixture is thick. Season with salt and pepper to taste and serve.

3 cups vegetable stock (page 20)

$1/2$ pound mushrooms (any variety), washed and diced

3 tablespoons cider vinegar

1 tablespoon soy sauce

$1/2$ teaspoon cayenne pepper

2 tablespoons cornstarch

1 tablespoon water

$1/2$ cup sliced bamboo strips, julienned

$1/2$ pound firm tofu, cut into $1/2$-inch pieces

1 large egg, beaten

Salt and freshly ground black pepper to taste

Lime Soup

1 tablespoon olive oil

1 medium red onion, diced

3 garlic cloves, minced

2 tablespoons dried oregano

Salt to taste

$^1/_2$ pound fried tofu

2 carrots, diced

$^1/_2$ pound green beans, cut
  into 1-inch pieces

2 medium tomatoes, diced

1 cup vegetable stock
  (page 20)

$^1/_2$ bunch of cilantro, finely
  chopped

2 tablespoons chili powder

2 limes, thinly sliced

Juice of 1 lime

I guess I really could have called this a "salsa soup." The mixture of herbs, onions, and tomatoes delivers a flavor very reminiscent of salsa. You citrus lovers should get a kick out of this one. Let me know what you think.

SERVES 2 TO 4

In a large pot, heat the oil and sauté the onion and garlic. Add the remaining ingredients and simmer until done, about 35 minutes.

Wild Mushroom Chowder

This chowder matches the richness and creaminess of clam or corn chowder, but the flavor varies tremendously depending on which mushrooms you use . . . strong and earthy from morels, delicate and flowerlike from chanterelles . . . it's a very versatile chowder.

SERVES 2 TO 4

Sauté the mushrooms and onions in the butter until the onions are translucent. Stir in the flour. Put this mixture into a medium saucepan along with the potatoes, thyme, pepper, and half-and-half. Cover and simmer for about 20 to 30 minutes. Stir frequently, taking care not to let the chowder burn. Serve it topped with the Italian parsley.

1 pound wild mushrooms, washed and diced

2 medium onions, diced

$^1/_2$ stick (2 ounces) butter

$^1/_4$ cup all-purpose flour

8 potatoes, peeled and diced

2 tablespoons dried thyme

Freshly ground black pepper to taste

4 cups half-and-half

$^1/_4$ cup fresh Italian parsley, chopped, for garnish

Pumpkin and Vegetable Chowder

〜〜〜〜〜

1 large onion, chopped

$^1/_4$ cup corn oil

1 tablespoon tamari sauce

1 ripe tomato, peeled and diced

4 cups vegetable stock (page 20)

4 cups pumpkin, puréed or in chunks

1 tablespoon maple syrup

Bunch of broccoli, steamed and coarsely chopped

$^1/_2$ cup heavy cream

Salt and freshly ground black pepper to taste

I've used broccoli in this chowder, but you can substitute your favorite vegetable or those that are in season.

SERVES 4 TO 6

In a large pot, cook the onion in the oil until it is translucent. Add the tamari sauce, tomato, stock, pumpkin, and maple syrup and combine well. Simmer for 30 minutes. Add the broccoli and cream and simmer another 10 to 15 minutes. Adjust the seasoning, adding salt and pepper to taste.

Corn Chowder

This is so good, it's hard to believe it's so easy to prepare. When I stopped eating red meat in the early eighties, hamburger was the only thing I truly missed. Veggie burgers helped take care of that. And when I gave up seafood a few years later, I really missed New England clam chowder. I'm able to quench my desire for that with corn chowder. It tastes nothing like clams, but it has the same feel and the same creaminess, and it's so filling.

SERVES 3 TO 5

Put the oil and butter in a large pot. Add the onion, shallot, and garlic and sauté until the onion is translucent, about 10 minutes. Add the stock, water, potato, celery, and bay leaf. Cook until the potato is tender, about 15 to 20 minutes. Add the corn, green onions, and milk. Lower the heat and simmer for 10 to 15 minutes. Season with salt and pepper. Remove the bay leaf and serve piping hot.

2 tablespoons corn oil

$^1/_4$ stick (1 ounce) butter

1 medium onion, diced

1 shallot, minced

1 garlic clove, minced

1 cup vegetable stock (page 20)

1 cup water

1 large potato, peeled and diced

1 celery stalk, diced

1 bay leaf

$2^1/_2$ cups corn, fresh, canned, or frozen

3 whole green onions, chopped

$^3/_4$ cup milk

Salt and freshly ground black pepper to taste

Black Bean Chili with Salsa

FOR THE CHILI

1 tablespoon olive oil

6 garlic cloves, crushed

1 large onion, chopped

1 green bell pepper, chopped

1 red bell pepper, chopped

1 pound black beans, soaked overnight and cooked

1 8-ounce can puréed tomatoes

1 1-pound can whole tomatoes, halved, with the juice retained

1 can green chiles

1 tablespoon ground cumin

1 tablespoon dried oregano

Cayenne pepper to taste

Juice of $1/2$ lime

FOR THE SALSA

2 red onions, diced

$1/2$ cup chopped cilantro

4 ripe tomatoes, diced

Juice of $1/2$ lime

$1/4$ cup chopped parsley

Black beans are fabulous when cooked with a little olive oil and onions. For chili, add some peppers and onions along with garlic. For a little more zing, add some fresh salsa as well.

SERVES 3 TO 5

Heat the olive oil in a large pan and sauté the garlic, onion, and green and red bell peppers. Add the black beans and the remaining ingredients. Season with salt and freshly ground black pepper if you want. Cover and simmer at least 1 hour and as much as 2 hours. While the chili is cooking, prepare the salsa.

Combine all the ingredients. Season with salt and freshly ground black pepper if you want. Dollop over the chili.

Vegetable Chili

Around my house, I refer to this as garden chili because in the summertime I just go outside and pull up onions, zucchini, yellow squash, tomatoes, and bell peppers to put in this dish. If you have any leftovers, add some rice and roll the whole mess up in tortillas to make wonderful burritos.

SERVES 3 TO 5

In a large pot, sauté the squash, zucchini, onions, garlic, and red and green bell peppers in the olive oil. Add the tomatoes, seasonings, kidney beans, garbanzo beans, dill, and lemon juice. Stir to mix well, cover, and simmer 45 to 50 minutes.

1 yellow squash, chopped

1 zucchini, chopped

2 yellow onions, diced

4 garlic cloves, crushed

1 red bell pepper, diced

1 green bell pepper, diced

$1/2$ cup olive oil

2 14-ounce cans plum Italian tomatoes, chopped, with the juice retained

1 pound fresh plum tomatoes

2 tablespoons chili powder

1 teaspoon ground cumin

1 tablespoon dried basil

1 tablespoon dried oregano

Salt and freshly ground black pepper to taste

$1/2$ cup fresh parsley, chopped

1 32-ounce can kidney beans, drained

1 32-ounce can garbanzo beans, drained

3 tablespoons fresh dill, chopped

Juice of $1/2$ lemon

White Chili

3 tablespoons olive oil or vegetable oil

1 large white onion, chopped

1 yellow bell pepper, chopped

1 pound potatoes, peeled and cut into chunks

2 garlic cloves, chopped

1 28-ounce can Italian stewed tomatoes, chopped, with the juice retained

1 16-ounce can cannellini beans, drained

1 cup vegetable stock (page 20)

1 6-ounce can tomato paste

2 tablespoons chili powder

2 teaspoons dried oregano

1 teaspoon red pepper flakes

Salt to taste

$1/2$ teaspoon freshly ground white pepper

$1/2$ cup chopped cilantro, for garnish

This is a very attractive chili, loaded with flavor. If you can't find cannellini beans, use baby limas or, as we call them in the South, butter beans. Also feel free to omit the red pepper flakes if you prefer a milder chili.

SERVES 3 TO 5

Heat the oil in a large pot. Sauté the onion, bell pepper, potatoes, and garlic until the vegetables are tender. Add the tomatoes, beans, stock, tomato paste, chili powder, oregano, red pepper flakes, salt, and white pepper. Combine well and simmer, covered, for about 30 to 40 minutes. Garnish each serving with chopped cilantro.

Okra *Thus far I haven't mentioned my struggles with literacy. Not because I haven't wanted to; it's just that there really hasn't been an appropriate spot in the book for it until now. Let me explain the tie-in between literacy and okra.*

In 1991, I received a box in the mail containing the first five copies of my first book, Guide to the Harvest. *You can understand the emotion I felt upon opening that box and seeing a book with my picture and name on the cover. Such moments must be emotional for any author, but for me, it was overwhelming. You see, until the age of twenty-six I was unable to read. And when I saw that book for the first time, I felt capable. I felt it really was possible to make my dreams a reality. I felt great. I felt literate.*

I picked the top book out of the box, randomly opened it, and looked down at the page. It had opened to the section about okra, and that was the first passage I read from my book. I'd like to share that passage with you, and after you read it, I think you will understand my love for okra.

The ancient vegetable, okra, a close relative of the cotton plant, originated in northeast Africa. I'm told it's not uncommon to see wild okra still growing today in Ethiopia and the upper Nile region.

Okra was, and still is, a staple in Africa, India, and the Mediterranean area. This unique vegetable was brought to America along with human cargo in the hulls of slave ships. Both ill-treated cargos survived harsh times in their new homeland and have made significant impacts on the culinary world.

In Africa, the words "okra" and "gumbo" are interchangeable. But in the United States, gumbo has come to mean a soup or stew associated with Creole cooking, and okra refers to the primary ingredient used in its preparation.

In my eyes, okra, with its spring-grass color and its intriguing cylindrical shape, is one of the most beautiful vegetables. I've often asked myself whether I feel this way because the history of this ancient food and my own cultural history are so closely intertwined.

I grew up eating okra, and my grandfather, W. H. Curtis, raised the best I've ever tasted. Each summer morning, he and I would inspect the plants (that looked so much like the cotton plants he spent his days with) and harvest the ripe vegetables. Then we'd take them in to my grandmother, Corine, who must have had fifty different ways to prepare the fruits (vegetables) of our labor: fried, boiled, cooked with onions or tomatoes in stews, pickled, or canned. If I had known then what I would be doing for a living, I would have written down everything Gramma did in her kitchen. Thank goodness my mama knows many of Gramma's secrets.

Stewed Okra and Tomatoes

When I prepare this dish, it takes me back to the days of being in the garden with Grandad. The flavor of the onion, tomato, and okra blend so well together. It's wonderful as a side dish, and great over corn bread or as a sauce on pizza.

SERVES 3 TO 4

Put all the ingredients into a medium pot, cover, and bring to a boil. Lower the heat and simmer, covered, for about 1 hour. This is great over corn bread, with cooked cabbage, beans, or greens, in soups, and even on pizza.

2 cups okra, cut into
  ¹/₂-inch pieces

2 large tomatoes, peeled
  and diced

1 medium onion, diced

4 tablespoons water

2 tablespoons sugar

Garden Vegetable Stew

1 large onion, chopped

3 garlic cloves, minced

3 carrots, chopped

2 summer squashes, chopped

$^1/_4$ cup vegetable oil

2 medium potatoes, peeled and diced

1 8-ounce can stewed tomatoes

4 cups vegetable stock (page 20)

2 cups sliced okra

3 cups corn kernels

1 cup lima beans

2 tablespoons Worcestershire sauce

3 tablespoons light brown sugar

2 tablespoons vinegar

3 tablespoons ketchup

1 tablespoon cornstarch

1 teaspoon water

Salt and freshly ground black pepper to taste

$^1/_4$ cup grated Swiss cheese, for garnish

This stew is a great anchor to any meal because it's so hearty and filling. You can serve it with just a salad and bread.

SERVES 4 TO 6

In a saucepan, sauté the onion, garlic, carrots, and squash in the oil until the vegetables are just tender. In a large stockpot, combine the sautéed vegetables with all the remaining ingredients except the cheese and bring to a boil. Lower the heat, cover, and simmer for about 1 hour. Sprinkle the cheese on top of each serving just before serving.

Note: If you like your stew with some spice to it, you can add some hot sauce with the ingredients as they simmer.

Potato Stew

If you're a potato lover, you can always add more potatoes to this stew. For thinner stew, add more of the cooking liquid from the lentils. The blend of lentils and potatoes along with the other vegetables makes for a flavor party in your pot.

SERVES 4 TO 6

In a saucepan, cook the lentils and bay leaf in the water for 20 to 30 minutes. Reduce the heat to medium and discard the bay leaf. In a big stockpot or Dutch oven, heat the butter and oil. Add the potatoes, tomatoes, turmeric, cayenne pepper, broth granules, garam masala, and honey. Cook about 8 to 12 minutes. Add the lentils with 2 cups of their cooking liquid (discard the remainder) and simmer, covered, for about 40 minutes. Cook an additional 10 minutes, uncovered, to thicken. Season with salt and pepper and serve.

1 cup lentils

1 bay leaf

5 cups water

1 tablespoon butter

2 tablespoons olive oil

3 large potatoes, peeled and cut into 1-inch cubes

2 8-ounce cans chopped tomatoes with their juice

1 teaspoon turmeric

Cayenne pepper to taste

1 teaspoon vegetable broth granules

2 teaspoons garam masala

1 tablespoon honey

Salt and freshly ground black pepper to taste

Veggie Stew

1 ounce dried shiitake
mushrooms, rehydrated
and chopped, or 1/2 pound
fresh shiitake mushrooms

3 shallots, chopped

1 tablespoon olive oil

1 pound carrots, cut into
1-inch chunks

1 pound potatoes, peeled
and cut into 1-inch cubes

1 bay leaf

1 tablespoon paprika

1/4 stick (1 ounce) butter

Salt and freshly ground black
pepper to taste

2 tablespoons chopped
fresh parsley

1 1/2 cups water

1 tablespoon all-purpose
flour

1/4 cup finely grated
Parmesan cheese, for
garnish

To me, stews are like a meal in a pot. Because I'm a wild mushroom fan, I can't help loving this dish—it's so thick and oniony and tasty!

SERVES 3 TO 5

Place the mushrooms and shallots in a large stockpot along with the olive oil and cook for 10 minutes. Add the carrots, potatoes, bay leaf, paprika, butter, salt and pepper, parsley, and water. Cover and cook over medium heat for about 30 minutes. Remove the lid and add the flour. Stir until the mixture begins to thicken and let it simmer for another 10 to 15 minutes. Remove the bay leaf. Sprinkle the grated Parmesan cheese over each serving and serve.

Salads and Dressings

Webster defines salad as "a cold dish... of raw vegetables, fruit, or meat served with dressing." That'll work, of course, but salad can be much more, right? I learned that as a child. I remember plenty of salads from when I was a kid: potato; macaroni, which hadn't become pasta yet to us Southerners, regardless of race; turnip; coleslaw, though I never truly regarded it as a salad; and fruit salad.

The one salad that really jumps out in my memory is the mainstay green salad. In those days, the most available lettuce in the South was iceberg. I loved iceberg lettuce then, and I still enjoy it, but on the nutrition scale it's far from the top. My mama compensated for the bland, sometimes watery flavor of iceberg lettuce salads by throwing in everything except the proverbial kitchen sink. She would shred two to three heads of iceberg, then go out back to the garden for fresh cucumbers, tomatoes, green onions, carrots, and bell peppers. "Eat as much as you want" was the rule. Like a lot of kids, I'd spend the next five minutes or so picking most of that stuff out of my salad. Then I'd smother whatever remained with plenty of Thousand Island dressing.

Looking back, I realize it was those salads that have given me the nerve to try all kinds of combinations as an adult, even though my preferences as a kid were a bit lim-

ited. I'd like to share some combinations I enjoy, as well as some information I've

learned about salad ingredients from my travels. We'll top them off with some interest-

ing dressings, intended more to enhance than to smother.

First, though, here are a few tips for shopping for fresh produce.

1. *Use your eyes.* Make sure the item looks good. If it doesn't look good, it prob-

ably isn't good. This is true of organic fruits and vegetables too.

2. *Use your nose.* When fruits are ripe, they smell ripe. Your produce counter can

smell as sweet as a rose garden. Mangoes, pineapples, oranges, and apples all give off

wonderful aromas when they are ripe. Ripe vegetables smell fresh, like the wonderful

scent of your yard after a spring rain. After a vegetable has passed its peak ripeness, it

smells sour.

3. *Use your hands.* Ripe fruits have a slight give to them when touched gently.

Try this experiment: Make a fist with your right hand, keeping your four fingers

curled into your palm. Bring your thumb up over your index finger in a tight clinch.

With the index finger of your left hand, press the tip of the thumb—not the nail, but the tip—on your right thumb. That's about how much give you should feel on a piece of ripe produce.

4. *Buy what is in season in your area.* Always start with local crops, then see what produce is available through regional or national distribution. Obviously, the closer the food is to you, the fresher it will be, so exhaust those possibilities before you buy imported produce.

5. *Get to know your produce person.* You can learn things about produce from this person that you'll never find out from reading a label.

These five steps to selecting fresh produce have almost become my trademark. It's useful, helpful information, and as easy as it sounds, it's information that bears repeating over and over. The day my first child, Curtis Jr., was due to be born, I was making a regular appearance on the Home Show. I was reminding the audience of these steps specifically regarding peaches, the fruit from my home state of Georgia. In the middle of the segment, I started laughing and couldn't stop. If that's ever happened to you, you'll understand the predicament I was in. Sarah Purcell, the show's co-host, began to laugh too, sensing that my mind wasn't quite on the matter at hand. She

managed to ask me what was going on, and I told her, "The baby's coming today!"
She hugged me and said, "You'd better finish up and get home!" So I looked at the
camera and said, "If it don't smell peachy, it ain't gonna taste peachy." That, in a
nutshell, is the key to selecting fresh produce.

Lettuce Salads
Many of us know about iceberg, romaine,
green and red leaf, and butter lettuces. They seem to have been with us forever and are
still the big sellers in markets from coast to coast. Over the past few years, dozens of
new lettuces have begun appearing, not only in restaurants and at fancy catered events,
but in our local markets as well. You can purchase some of these lettuces in the form of
salad mixes. Sometimes they're called "baby salad mix" or "seasonal salad mix."
Eventually, they will be available for purchase as whole heads. Always remember to
avoid any lettuce that has wilted or yellowing leaves. Turn the head upside down, and
press the core. A soft core means old lettuce. That's true of the more traditional lettuces
as well as for the newer varieties. Here are a few of the newer lettuces to look for.

Green Oak: The leaf looks very much like the leaf of the Southern oak tree and *has a distinct, earthy flavor.*

Red Oak: The leaf looks more like that of the scrub oak found in northern California. The color varies from white to light green in the center and it has a red tip. It has a milder and sweeter flavor than the green oak.

Lollo Rossa: This leaf is so beautiful it could be used in flower arrangements. The color pattern is much like that of the red oak, but the tip of the leaf is ruffled.

Red Butter: A variety of Boston lettuce, red butter looks exactly like its namesake, except the leaf has a reddish tinge. The taste, believe it or not, is even better.

Red Romaine: The color gives a Caesar salad a new look with the same great flavor.

Red Perella: In appearance, this is almost a twin to Bibb lettuce, but red.

Spinach and Kale Salad

A member of the cabbage family, kale is often used as decoration. What a waste. This vegetable is loaded with vitamins A and C . . . plus it tastes great when cooked. This dish is especially good with pasta.

SERVES 4

Heat the oil in a pan and cook the red bell pepper, garlic, and kale about 5 minutes, covered. Add the spinach and salt and black pepper and cook about 5 minutes more. Stir in the balsamic vinegar. Serve hot.

2 tablespoons olive oil

1 red bell pepper, diced

2 garlic cloves, diced

Bunch of kale, chopped

Bunch of spinach, chopped

Salt and freshly ground black pepper to taste

4 tablespoons balsamic vinegar

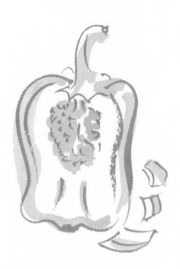

Caesar Salad

Head of romaine, torn apart,
cut up, or chopped

2 garlic cloves, chopped

6 tablespoons olive oil

4 tablespoons lemon juice

2 tablespoons Worcestershire
sauce

2 hard-boiled eggs, mashed

6 tablespoons Parmesan
cheese, grated

1 recipe Homemade Croutons
(page 61)

I have a hard time trying any other kind of salad in a restaurant when a Caesar salad is also on the menu. And, of course, every restaurant has its own version. My favorite restaurant Caesar salad is served at the Hilltop Cafe in Marin County, California. My second favorite, believe it or not, is available near the San Francisco area of the food court at Universal Studios in Orlando, Florida. Here's my homemade version.

SERVES 4

Place the romaine in a large wooden salad bowl. In a mixing bowl, combine the garlic, olive oil, lemon juice, Worcestershire sauce, egg, and cheese. Mix well and pour over the greens. Toss and serve with homemade croutons.

Wilted Salad for Two

This is one of those recipes I originally made just for myself. Though I easily could eat the entire salad, I realized I always made enough for two . . . and besides, it's so good, it should be shared.

SERVES 2

Place the greens in a salad bowl. In a saucepan, sauté the onion in the oil for about 2 minutes, then add the remaining ingredients. Bring to a boil and pour over the lettuce greens. Toss and serve.

2 to 3 cups greens of your choice, torn into pieces

$1/2$ small onion, diced

$1/4$ cup vegetable oil

2 tablespoons white vinegar

$1/2$ teaspoon ground mustard

$1/8$ teaspoon garlic salt

$1/2$ teaspoon sugar

Salt and freshly ground black pepper to taste

Homemade Croutons

Why buy 'em when you can make 'em? Wow! . . . these are great!

Melt the butter in a sauté pan. Add the bread. Sprinkle the garlic salt and herbs on top of the bread. Toss the bread pieces constantly until all the butter has been absorbed.

$1/2$ stick (2 ounces) butter, melted

3 slices day-old bread, toasted and broken into bite-size pieces

$1/2$ teaspoon garlic salt

$1/4$ teaspoon dried rosemary

$1/4$ teaspoon dried sage

$1/4$ teaspoon dried thyme

Turnip Salad

Bunch of turnip greens

1 cup water

$^1/_4$ cup corn oil

Salt and freshly ground black pepper to taste

1 hot pepper, chopped (optional)

1 green bell pepper, chopped (optional)

What most of America calls turnip greens is known as turnip salad in the South. The turnip plant has two edible parts: the root or bulb, which cooks up into a pretty darn good vegetable itself, and the green tops. My first hot salad was turnip salad, and though it is a classic soul food dish, as a kid I really didn't much care for it. And like most Southern cooks, Mama prepared turnip greens with pork or pork fat.

This is my update on Mama's greens to suit my new meat-free lifestyle.

You can serve this dish with sliced tomatoes and onions, but even though it's called a salad, this is one salad that isn't served as a first course. It's always been a side dish in our house, accompanied by plenty of hot corn bread.

SERVES 3 TO 4

Take at least 1 mess, which is what a bunch of greens is called in the South, and wash it thoroughly. Remove the large stem that runs through the center of each leaf. (If you fold the leaf lengthwise along the stem, you can pull the whole stem out at once.) Tear the leaves into pieces and place them in a large pot. Add the water, oil, salt and black pepper. Bring the greens to a boil, then cover them and reduce the heat. Simmer them for about 1 hour. Adjust the seasoning by adding more salt and pepper if necessary. Sometimes Mama will add a chopped hot or green bell pepper for additional flavor. Try it and see what you think.

Georgia-Florida Salad

This is an unusual salad making use of some of my favorite produce from Georgia and Florida. The flavor of a Vidalia onion is so sweet you can eat it like an apple. After you try this salad, write me and let me know what you think.

SERVES 4

Toss all the ingredients together in a large salad bowl. Serve chilled.

1 Vidalia onion, thinly sliced

1 orange, peeled and thinly sliced

3 cups mixed lettuce leaves, torn into pieces

$^1/_2$ cup chopped pecans

$^1/_2$ cup fresh strawberries, halved or quartered

$^1/_4$ to $^1/_2$ cup French Dressing (page 82)

Mama's Potato Salad

2 dozen small new potatoes, peeled and halved

4 hard-boiled eggs, chopped

1 to 2 celery stalks, finely diced

1 medium onion, diced

2 tablespoons chopped pimiento

3 tablespoons sweet relish

4 to 5 tablespoons mayonnaise

1 tablespoon yellow mustard

1/2 teaspoon salt

1/2 teaspoon freshly ground black pepper

1/2 teaspoon sugar

The first Sunday in September is Homecoming at my church, Rock Temple AME. If you are ever in Conyers, Georgia, Sunday school is at 9:45 A.M., and church services begin at 11:00 A.M. every Sunday. Consider yourself invited. Homecoming is always a great day of church. It's a morning when the Lord's house is full of people and His praises and it continues in the afternoon with the best potato salad party anywhere around. Homecoming is one of those occasions that hasn't changed much for me since I was a kid. I sample every mother's potato salad, just like I did back then, and after eating some of every salad, I always come back to the table for the best—my mama's. Some things never change. This is a variation of one of Mama's potato salads.

SERVES 6 PLUS

Boil the potatoes for about 20 minutes, or until they are tender, and allow them to cool. In a large bowl, combine the remaining ingredients. Mix and chill before serving.

Macaroni Salad

As a kid I thought macaroni salad and potato salad had nothing in common except their last name. I was also convinced that it must be really hard to make a great macaroni salad. You can imagine how floored I was years later when Mama informed me there's nothing to it. Using her basic potato salad recipe, all she does is switch macaroni for the potatoes—the rest of the recipe remains the same.

SERVES 6 PLUS

Boil the macaroni until barely done and allow it to cool. In a large bowl, combine the remaining ingredients. Mix and chill before serving.

1 to 1^1/$_2$ pounds macaroni

4 hard-boiled eggs, chopped

1 to 2 celery stalks, finely diced

1 medium onion, diced

2 tablespoons chopped pimiento

3 tablespoons sweet relish

4 to 5 tablespoons mayonnaise

1 tablespoon yellow mustard

^{1}/$_2$ teaspoon salt

^{1}/$_2$ teaspoon freshly ground black pepper

^{1}/$_2$ teaspoon sugar

Pasta and Grape Salad

FOR THE SALAD

1 1/2 cups red and green grapes, mixed

1 cup diced fresh fruit of your choice

1 whole green onion, thinly sliced

1 ripe avocado, peeled and diced

Grilled vegetables of your choice

Salad greens of your choice

4 ounces bow tie pasta, cooked

FOR THE DRESSING

1/3 cup sour cream or plain yogurt

2 tablespoons white grape juice

2 tablespoons grapeseed oil or other vegetable oil

1 tablespoon sugar

1/2 tablespoon ground cinnamon

1/4 teaspoon paprika

This is a great cold salad. Before I served this to my family, they thought I was crazy to put fruit with pasta. After eating it, though, and enjoying the refreshing, cool, sweet flavors of the fruit combined with the grilled vegetables and bow tie pasta, they changed their minds and now ask for it often. I'm sure you will be pleasantly surprised with this combination.

SERVES 4 TO 6

In a large salad bowl, mix all the salad ingredients together. Mix together all the ingredients for the dressing in a small bowl and pour over the salad. Serve the salad well chilled.

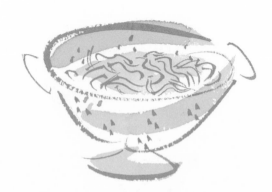

Coleslaw

This is another favorite dish Mama served with fish on Fridays. In my coleslaw I use a delicious mixture of cabbage, carrot, pepper, and onion, along with sweet relish and lemon juice, which add a sweet-sour flavor. Coleslaw is not just a Southern tradition anymore, it's become a favorite across the nation.

SERVES 6

Mix all the ingredients together, chill, and serve.

1 medium cabbage, grated

1 onion, grated

1 carrot, grated

1 green bell pepper, chopped

2 tablespoons sweet relish

$1/_2$ cup mayonnaise

$1/_2$ teaspoon lemon juice

$1/_2$ teaspoon white vinegar

Carrot Slaw

Carrots are a wonderful vegetable. Not only do they help your eyes, they also help your bones. My two-and-a-half-year-old son loves this salad and I bet your children will too. If they think it is too sour, just cut back on the vinegar and add a bit more sugar. The benefits derived from the carrots far outweigh the extra sugar.

SERVES 4

Mix all the ingredients together. This can be served at room temperature or chilled.

10 carrots, grated

$1/_2$ cup light sour cream

$1/_3$ cup mayonnaise

1 tablespoon cider vinegar

1 teaspoon balsamic vinegar

1 tablespoon sugar

$1/_2$ teaspoon salt

$1/_4$ cup fresh chives

Parsnip Salad

1 parsnip, grated

¹/₂ small Vidalia onion, finely diced

1 to 2 celery stalks, chopped

6 ripe or green olives, chopped (each kind imparts its own different flavor)

2 cups salad greens, torn into pieces

¹/₄ cup Tarragon Dressing (page 80) plus more if desired

2 tablespoons mayonnaise

The parsnip is one of those old-timey vegetables many of us seem to have forgotten. Whenever I prepare this salad for friends, they always want to know what the special flavor is. Of course, it's the grated parsnips. Parsnips, by the way, look just like carrots, except they're white.

SERVES 3 TO 4

Place the parsnip, onion, celery, olives, and salad greens in a salad bowl. Mix the tarragon dressing with the mayonnaise and pour the dressing over the greens. Toss well.

Lentil Salad

Lentils are wonderful. Unlike other types of beans, these cook quickly without the necessity of soaking overnight.

SERVES 4 TO 6

Place all the ingredients in a salad bowl and toss to mix.

In a small bowl, whisk together the mustard, vinegar, and oil. Season with salt and pepper and pour over the salad. Toss to coat the salad.

FOR THE SALAD

2 cups cooked lentils

$^3/_4$ cup chopped green onions

1 red bell pepper, chopped

$^1/_2$ cup chopped parsley

$^1/_4$ cup pine nuts

$^1/_4$ cup peanuts

$^1/_4$ cup walnuts

FOR THE DRESSING

1 teaspoon Dijon mustard

$^1/_4$ cup red wine vinegar

$^1/_3$ cup olive oil

Salt and freshly ground black pepper to taste

Lentil-Vinaigrette Salad

2 cups cooked lentils

1 pound smoked tofu

$1/2$ to $3/4$ cup French Dressing (page 82)

$1/4$ cup fresh parsley, chopped

Salt and freshly ground black pepper to taste

2 hard-boiled eggs, chopped

If you don't want to cook lentils for this recipe, just use canned beans of any kind and remember to rinse them well. And, if you can't find smoked tofu, just throw regular tofu on the grill, or fry it quickly in a sauté pan.

SERVES 4 TO 6

Combine all the ingredients in a large mixing bowl, toss, and serve.

Bean Salad

This is a wonderful bean salad. You can even reduce the amount of olive oil without weakening the flavor of the dish.

SERVES 6

In a large mixing bowl, combine the olive oil, lime juice, cilantro, cumin, and salt and pepper. Add the remaining ingredients and toss until the mixture is thoroughly blended.

$^1/_2$ cup olive oil

$^1/_3$ cup freshly squeezed lime juice

$^1/_4$ cup chopped cilantro

1 teaspoon ground cumin

Salt and freshly ground black pepper to taste

2 cups lima beans, cooked

1 cup black beans, cooked

1 cup red kidney beans, cooked

$^1/_2$ green bell pepper, chopped

$^1/_2$ red bell pepper, chopped

1 cup chopped red onion

2 cups sweet corn kernels

Quick Avocado-Vinaigrette Salad

1/2 cup watercress leaves

1/2 cup arugula leaves

2 ripe avocados, halved, pitted, and peeled

1/4 cup minced red onion

1/2 cup tomatoes, seeded and diced

2 tablespoons chopped fresh basil

Juice of 1/2 lemon

2 teaspoons red wine vinegar

1/3 cup olive oil

Salt and freshly ground black pepper to taste

The watercress and arugula in this salad provide a refreshing tangy contrast to the rich, creamy texture of the avocado. It is a wonderful, easy salad and beautiful to serve.

SERVES 4

Cover a platter with the watercress and arugula. Place the avocado facedown on the greens. Slice the avocado crosswise and fan it out across the greens. Thoroughly mix the remaining ingredients and pour over the avocado and greens.

Avocado and Salsa Salad

〜〜〜

This versatile dish is a salad, a gazpacho or cold soup, or a dip and can be served with a fork, a spoon, or chips.

SERVES 4 TO 6

Combine all the ingredients and purée them in a blender or food processor.

2 ripe avocados, pitted, peeled, and julienned

2 ripe tomatoes, peeled, seeded, and chopped

$1/4$ cup finely chopped onion

2 garlic cloves, minced

1 to 2 tablespoons hot pepper, diced

$1/3$ cup chopped fresh cilantro leaves

$1/3$ cup fresh lime juice

$1/3$ cup olive oil

1 teaspoon ground cumin

2 cups milk

Salt and freshly ground black pepper to taste

Asparagus and Sautéed Vegetable Salad

Head of iceberg lettuce, shredded

$^1/_4$ cup olive oil

3 garlic cloves, minced

1 tablespoon grated gingerroot

$^1/_2$ red bell pepper, diced

$^1/_2$ yellow bell pepper, diced

$^1/_2$ pound tofu

$^1/_2$ pound eggplant, cubed

$^1/_4$ cup dry white wine

$^1/_4$ cup vegetable stock (page 20)

1 pound asparagus, cut into 1-inch pieces and steamed (about 4 to 5 minutes)

2 tablespoons fresh parsley

Some consider iceberg lettuce bland. And even though it's not the best lettuce for you, I love it, especially with just a little Thousand Island dressing and tomatoes. This dish is a great accompaniment to pasta or rice.

SERVES 4

Arrange the lettuce on a large platter. Heat half the oil in a saucepan and add the garlic, ginger, peppers, and tofu. Cover and cook 4 minutes. Add the remaining oil and eggplant. Cook, uncovered, an additional 3 minutes. Add the white wine and stock. Stir with a wooden spoon until the liquid is reduced, about 3 to 5 minutes. Mix in the asparagus and parsley. Serve on the iceberg lettuce.

Broccoli Salad

Broccoli, one of the more popular members of the cabbage family, is loaded with vitamins, minerals, and fiber. Here's a recipe that takes advantage of all the goodness broccoli offers.

SERVES 4

Blanch the broccoli, mushrooms, onion, and celery. Drain and put in a salad bowl. In another bowl, mix together the remaining ingredients, stirring to combine well. Pour the dressing over the broccoli mixture.

$1^1/_2$ pounds fresh broccoli florets, cut into bite-sized pieces

$^1/_2$ pound mushrooms, wild or white, sliced

1 small red onion, sliced into thin rings

1 celery stalk, chopped

1 cup vegetable oil

$^1/_2$ cup white wine vinegar

$^1/_4$ cup sugar

1 tablespoon Italian seasoning

2 teaspoons dry mustard

Salt and freshly ground black pepper to taste

Asian Cucumber Salad

~~~~~~

3 cucumbers, peeled and
thinly sliced

3 tablespoons soy sauce

1 cup rice wine vinegar

1 tablespoon sesame oil

2 whole green onions,
chopped

1 tablespoon grated
fresh ginger

$^1/_2$ teaspoon salt

1 tablespoon sugar

I find a version of this recipe at many Asian restaurants in the San Francisco area. I'm always amazed that a dish that looks so thin can deliver so much flavor. The soy and vinegar pull all the flavor from the vegetables, and that little dash of sugar keeps the dressing from being bitter.

SERVES 4 TO 6

Place the cucumbers in a bowl. In another bowl, mix the remaining ingredients, stirring to combine well. Pour the sauce over the cucumbers.

Cauliflower Salad

This is a quick and easy recipe with the dressing made right alongside the salad. It's a two-in-one dish.

SERVES 4

Combine the cauliflower and olives in a serving bowl. In a small bowl, mix together the remaining ingredients to make a dressing. Pour the dressing over the cauliflower and olives and toss. This can be served either chilled or at room temperature.

1 pound cauliflower florets, cut into bite-sized pieces, and slightly steamed or blanched

$1/2$ cup green olives

$1/2$ cup pitted black olives

2 tablespoons minced red onion

1 tablespoon minced green bell pepper

2 tablespoons Dijon mustard

$1/4$ cup olive oil

2 tablespoons red wine vinegar

Salt and freshly ground black pepper to taste

Waldorf Salad

3 cups cored and diced
apples (Use the apples of
your choice—Red Delicious,
Rome Beauty, and Granny
Smith are my preferences.)

1 cup diced celery

$1/2$ to $3/4$ cup chopped
pecans

$1/2$ cup mayonnaise

When I was a kid, Dad, my brothers, and I would travel up to the mountains every fall for the sole purpose of bringing home baskets of freshly picked country apples. Mama used them in many dishes, but on special occasions and sometimes on Sunday, she would use them to make Waldorf salad. I didn't find out this was a classy salad until I became an adult. I don't think Mama knew it either.

SERVES 4 TO 6

Mix all the ingredients in a bowl. Chill and serve on a bed of lettuce.

Stuffed Avocado with Cilantro Mayonnaise

~~~

I call avocados my California fruit because I had never eaten one until I visited California in the eighties. And I absolutely love the creamy, buttery texture and flavor of this nonsweet fruit.

SERVES 4 TO 6

Dice the avocado pulp. Combine the pulp with the tomatoes, onion, and olives and mix well. Fill the avocado shells with the avocado mixture. Prepare the cilantro mayonnaise.

Combine all the ingredients and mix well. Dollop the cilantro mayonnaise on top of each stuffed avocado half. Store the remaining mayonnaise in the refrigerator for up to 1 week.

FOR THE AVOCADO STUFFING

2 to 3 ripe avocados, halved, pitted, and the pulp removed

2 tomatoes, diced

1 small onion, diced

7 ripe olives, chopped

FOR THE CILANTRO MAYONNAISE

$1/2$ cup mayonnaise

$1/2$ cup sour cream

2 tablespoons chopped fresh cilantro leaves

2 tablespoons fresh parsley (Italian or regular), chopped

Zest of 1 small orange

Juice of $1/2$ orange

Salt and freshly ground black pepper to taste

Tarragon Dressing

～○～○～

2 tablespoons finely chopped
  fresh tarragon

4 tablespoons salad oil

1¹/₂ tablespoons vinegar

³/₄ teaspoon salt

1 to 2 garlic cloves, minced

Dash of finely ground black
  pepper

After moving to California, I fell in love with this licorice-flavored herb.

MAKES ¹/₄ PLUS CUP (AND GOES A LONG WAY)

Mix all the ingredients in a bowl or jar, and stir or shake to mix. Serve over salad greens and steamed vegetables.

Sweet Salad Dressing

～○～○～

¹/₂ cup strawberry jelly

¹/₄ cup salad oil or
  nut-flavored oil

3 tablespoons lime juice

¹/₂ garlic clove, squeezed
  through garlic press

This dressing tastes great with Napa cabbage or drizzled over citrus salads, such as orange and grapefruit slices.

MAKES A VERY SCANT CUP

Combine all the ingredients and mix with a whisk or in a blender until smooth.

Coleslaw Dressing

Use this dressing with cabbage or lettuce greens.

Coleslaw dressing is not just for coleslaw anymore. This one can be used on any salad: lettuce leaves, sliced tomatoes, even mozzarella cheese! The sour cream and egg make it creamy, which is what makes a great coleslaw.

MAKES ABOUT 1/2 CUP

1/2 cup sour cream

1 large egg yolk

1 1/2 tablespoons vinegar

1 tablespoon sugar

1/2 teaspoon dry mustard

1/4 teaspoon dill seeds

Cook all the ingredients in a saucepan over medium heat. Stir constantly until the mixture thickens. Keep refrigerated.

Fruit Dressing

This dressing is for when I have to cheat. One of my five laws for buying produce is always buy what is in season. However, every now and again, we come across some unripened, unsweetened fruit which needs a little help, and this dressing does the trick. A bit of this dressing added to a stir-fry, along with some soy sauce, ain't bad either!

MAKES ABOUT 2 1/2 CUPS

2 large eggs, well beaten

Juice of 2 oranges

Grated rind of 1/2 orange

Juice of 2 lemons

Grated rind of 1/2 lemon

Juice of 2 limes

Grated rind of 1/2 lime

1 1/2 cups sugar

In a saucepan, bring all the ingredients to a boil. Remove from heat while stirring to combine and dissolve the sugar. Cool and serve over fruit.

French Dressing

1/2 cup vegetable oil or olive oil

2 tablespoons vinegar

2 tablespoons lemon juice

Dash of dry mustard

Dash of paprika

This is an easy variation of the classic French dressing. I know most Americans think of French dressing as a pink dressing made with mayonnaise, but in truth, classic French dressings are vinaigrettes. Vinaigrettes, by the way, are considered one of the five "mother sauces." By adding a little of this or that, you can customize your dressing to suit your taste and palate.

MAKES ABOUT 3/4 CUP

Combine all the ingredients in a jar with a tightly fitting lid. Shake well to mix just before serving. Keep refrigerated.

Easy Blue Cheese Dressing

1/3 cup crumbled Saga blue cheese

1/4 teaspoon Worcestershire sauce

1 recipe French Dressing (above)

While living in New York City, I grew to love Scandinavian cheese. It's tough to pick a favorite, but one I especially enjoy is Saga. The texture is creamy smooth, and it has a nice tang from the blue cheese.

MAKES ABOUT 1 CUP

In a bowl, add the blue cheese and Worcestershire sauce to the French dressing. Mix well to combine. Keep refrigerated.

Tartar Sauce

~~~~~~

Mama always made this on Fridays to go with fish, but it's also pretty good on salad. She made two versions, one with minced dill, the other with chopped, sweet pickles. The pickle version is my favorite. Try both and see which you prefer.

MAKES ABOUT 1 1/2 CUPS

In a bowl, combine all the ingredients and mix well. Keep refrigerated.

1 cup mayonnaise

1/4 small onion, finely diced

2 teaspoons chopped pimiento

2 heaping tablespoons minced fresh dill or 2 heaping tablespoons chopped sweet pickles

One-of-Many Thousand Island Dressing

~~~~~~

I used to smother my green salads in Thousand Island dressing. Try my two versions of this classic dressing, and you'll know why.

MAKES ABOUT 1 3/4 CUPS

Mix all the ingredients together in a bowl, pour on salad greens, and enjoy.

1 cup mayonnaise

2 tablespoons chili sauce

3 stuffed green olives, chopped

1 whole green onion, chopped

2 hard-boiled eggs, finely chopped

1/2 teaspoon paprika

Another Thousand Island Dressing

1 cup mayonnaise

Scant $^1/_2$ cup ketchup

$^1/_4$ small onion, finely diced

2 tablespoons finely diced
  red bell pepper

2 tablespoons finely diced
  green bell pepper

2 tablespoons sweet
  pickle relish

1 hard-boiled egg, mashed

Dash of salt and finely ground
  black pepper

Light cream if needed

MAKES ABOUT 2 CUPS

In a bowl, mix together all the ingredients except the cream. If the dressing isn't thick enough, add the cream, 1 teaspoon at a time, until thickened.

Country Buttermilk Dressing

You can do so many wonderful things to buttermilk dressing. To enhance the flavor, add about two tablespoons of fresh herbs such as oregano, basil, and thyme. When using dried herbs, decrease the amount to one to one and a half teaspoons each, and add the herbs directly to the buttermilk. Let stand for about 10 minutes before completing the dressing. You can also add about ten ounces of crumbled blue cheese. I like Saga, but any kind of blue cheese will do.

1 1/2 cups buttermilk

1 small onion, finely chopped

2 garlic cloves, minced

1 cup mayonnaise

Salt and freshly ground black pepper to taste

MAKES ABOUT 3 CUPS

Combine all the ingredients in a bowl and mix well.

Blue Cheese Dressing

There are two blue cheese dressing recipes in this book. The other one on page 82 is an easy, milder version. This one has a little more zing.

1 cup sour cream

1/2 tablespoon lemon juice

1/4 teaspoon Worcestershire sauce

1 garlic clove, minced

4 ounces or more blue cheese, crumbled (Saga or an American blue cheese)

MAKES ABOUT 1 1/2 CUPS

In a bowl, mix all the ingredients together, stirring well to combine.

Onion Dressing

1¹/₂ cups finely chopped onion (a mixture of red, green, and yellow onions really makes this dressing special)

3 garlic cloves, minced

2 tablespoons vinegar

2 tablespoons spicy mustard

1 cup mayonnaise

1 to 1¹/₂ cups sour cream

Dash of freshly ground black pepper

Onion dressing is great on vegetable salads, especially hot ones, such as sautéed sweet peppers, or steamed broccoli and cauliflower. It's also wonderful with cold vegetables, such as artichokes or asparagus.

MAKES ABOUT 4 CUPS

In a bowl, combine all the ingredients and mix well. If you prefer a smoother dressing, place the onions, garlic, vinegar, and mustard in a blender and purée them before adding them to the other ingredients.

Lunches, Brunches, and Other Light Meals

Veggie Burgers 1

2 cups beans (any variety), cooked

2 to 3 tablespoons cracked wheat

2 tablespoons cottage cheese or sour cream

2 tablespoons chopped green onions

1 tablespoon chopped fresh parsley

$1/2$ teaspoon ground cumin

Salt and freshly ground black pepper to taste

$1/4$ cup peanut oil, for frying (optional)

Serve these on buns and enjoy them just as you would a hamburger.

SERVES 4

Place all the ingredients except the oil in a food processor or blender and purée. Place the purée in a medium-size mixing bowl, cover with plastic wrap, and refrigerate for 30 to 40 minutes until it is cool and firm. Just before cooking, remove the mixture from the refrigerator and shape into burger patties. The patties can be fried in the peanut oil, $3\frac{1}{2}$ to 4 minutes per side, or they can be baked in a 350°F oven for 25 minutes.

Mushroom Burgers or Veggie Burgers 2

This is another one of my meatless burger recipes. These take a bit more time than Veggie Burger 1, but you'll love them just as much.

SERVES 4 TO 6

In a saucepan, combine the celery, garlic, garlic powder, onion, Italian seasoning, and marjoram, and sauté in the olive oil. Add the mushrooms and cook until the liquid evaporates. In a mixing bowl, combine the barley, oats, sunflower seeds, pecans, sesame paste, and soy sauce with the sautée mixture. Mix all the ingredients thoroughly, then cover the bowl with plastic wrap and chill. Just before cooking, remove the mixture from the refrigerator and shape into patties. The patties can be fried in the peanut oil, 3½ to 4 minutes per side, or they can be baked in a 350°F oven for 25 minutes.

1 celery stalk, diced

4 garlic cloves, crushed or minced

1 teaspoon garlic powder

1 medium onion, diced

2 teaspoons Italian seasoning

1 teaspoon ground marjoram

1 tablespoon olive oil

1 pound mushrooms of your choice, washed and chopped

1 cup cooked barley

1 cup cooked rolled oats

$1/2$ cup sunflower seeds, toasted

$1/4$ cup pecans, toasted, or any other kind of nuts

$1/4$ cup sesame paste

2 tablespoons soy sauce

$1/4$ cup peanut oil, for frying (optional)

Tofu and Cheese Burgers or Veggie Burgers 3

1/2 green bell pepper, minced

1/2 medium onion, minced

2 teaspoons olive oil

1 pound extra-firm tofu, drained and crumbled

2 tablespoons whole wheat flour

2 tablespoons soy sauce

2 large eggs, beaten

1/2 cup shredded cheese (any variety)

Salt and freshly ground black pepper to taste

15 saltine crackers, crumbled

1/4 cup peanut oil, for frying (optional)

These delicious burgers are somewhat wet when prepared. Use the cracker crumbs to coat the patties. Not only do the crumbs help absorb the excess moisture, they also help hold the burgers together.

SERVES 4 TO 6

In a saucepan, sauté the green bell pepper and onion in the olive oil and let cool. In a mixing bowl, combine the tofu, flour, soy sauce, eggs, cheese, and salt and pepper. Add the cooled green pepper and onion to the mixture and stir. Cover the bowl with plastic wrap and place in the refrigerator until the mixture is thoroughly chilled. Form patties and coat them with the cracker crumbs. The patties can be fried in the peanut oil, 3½ to 4 minutes per side; they can be baked in a 350°F oven for 25 minutes; or they can be broiled until golden brown on both sides.

Grated Vegetable Patties with Wine Sauce

Because I am constantly on the road, I eat out frequently. Oftentimes I forget the names of the restaurants, but I never forget a truly great dish. This is my version of a vegetable patty I had in New York City . . . can't remember the name of the restaurant, but, oh! those patties. I'll never forget them. Try my version with gravy or puréed fruit sauce, or serve them cold.

SERVES 3 TO 4

Preheat the oven to 350°F. In a large bowl, to the grated vegetables, add the eggs, flour, and seasonings. Combine all the ingredients well. Turn the mixture into a greased and floured cake pan and bake about 1½ hours, or until the patty is crusty brown. Cut it into slices and serve them with the wine sauce.

1 large carrot, grated

¹/₂ large turnip, peeled and grated

1 large potato, peeled and grated

1 medium sweet potato, peeled and grated

¹/₂ small onion, grated

2 large eggs, slightly beaten

2 tablespoons all-purpose flour

¹/₂ teaspoon salt

¹/₄ teaspoon freshly ground black pepper

¹/₄ teaspoon dried sage

¹/₄ teaspoon dried thyme

Wine Sauce (page 92)

Wine Sauce

4 whole green onions,
  chopped

1 tablespoon olive oil

$^1/_2$ cup dry white wine

2 tablespoons lemon juice

Salt and freshly ground black
  pepper to taste

$^1/_2$ teaspoon dried oregano

$^1/_2$ teaspoon dried
  tarragon

1 tablespoon cornstarch

Grated Vegetable Patties
  (page 91)

This sauce is great over grilled or roasted vegetables.

MAKES 1 CUP

In a saucepan, sauté the green onions in the oil, wine, and lemon juice for 5 to 7 minutes. Season with salt and pepper and the herbs. Thicken the sauce with the cornstarch. Serve over vegetable patties.

White Bean Cakes

These can be used very much like veggie burgers or served as you would egg foo yung with a nice vegetable gravy (page 164).

SERVES 6

Place the beans, garlic, green onions, cilantro, cumin, coriander, baking powder, egg yolk, flour, and salt and pepper in a blender or food processor. Process until thoroughly combined. While the oil is heating in a frying pan, form the bean mixture into patties. Fry the patties in the hot oil until brown on both sides, 3½ to 4 minutes per side.

3 cups cannellini beans, cooked and drained

2 garlic cloves, chopped

4 whole green onions, chopped

2 tablespoons chopped fresh cilantro

1 tablespoon ground cumin

1 tablespoon ground coriander

1 tablespoon baking powder

1 large egg yolk

1 cup all-purpose flour

Salt and freshly ground black pepper, to taste

¼ cup canola oil, for frying, plus more if necessary

Grilled Vegetables

1 large onion, sliced

2 zucchini, sliced

2 yellow squashes, sliced

1 eggplant, sliced

$^1/_2$ cup soy sauce

Juice of 2 medium oranges

Vegetables have been a part of my diet all of my life, and in the South during my youth, vegetables were generally prepared one of two ways: boiled or fried. Don't get me wrong, I love vegetables cooked in those traditional ways, but living in California, I've been introduced to other ways of preparing vegetables: roasting, steaming, sautéing, and grilling.

In my opinion, the key to making great grilled vegetables is to marinate them. This not only adds flavor to the vegetables, but it also keeps them from drying out completely during the cooking process.

I came up with this recipe on a day we were headed to the beach with little Curtis. Let me set the stage: towels, buckets, shovels, umbrella, BBQ grill, cooler, food, one fifteen-pound baby, fifty pounds of baby gear. Sound familiar? After some clever shifting around of things, I was able to fit everything into the car, and as you will see, I even figured out how to keep the sand out of the food. But how do you keep the sand out of the baby? Now that little Curtis is a big brother to baby Cole, you'll need to write me with your suggestions on how to keep the sand out of the baby.

In the meantime, you'll enjoy this recipe. It's a fun one to cook outside on the grill, whether at home, in a park, or at the beach. Just put a cup and a half or so of each of the vegetables to be grilled into a plastic bag along with the marinade. Seal the bag tightly, and by the time you've arrived at your picnic destination and the grill is hot, the vegetables will be perfectly marinated. As always, feel free to use any combination of vegetables you like.

Combine all the sliced vegetables except the eggplant in an airtight plastic bag. If you marinate the eggplant with the other vegetables, it will absorb all the liquid, so marinate the eggplant separately in another bag. Mix the soy sauce and orange juice together and pour over the vegetables and seal the bags. Marinate at least 30 minutes.

Place the vegetables on a vegetable rack (a fairly inexpensive rack made especially for BBQ grills that prevents vegetables from falling through the grill) or on tinfoil into which holes have been punched and place them on the grill. Cook until the vegetables are tender, which depends upon how hot your grill is. You can also wrap the vegetables in tinfoil, place the foil packet on the grill, and steam the vegetables.

Veggie Melt

Hamburger buns, onion rolls, sliced bread (your choice)

$1/2$ cup grilled or steamed vegetables per sandwich

2 ounces any variety cheese, grated or sliced, per sandwich

This is another spectacular way to enjoy grilled or steamed vegetables. The combination of vegetables and cheese, heated until all the flavors are joined, will make you come back for more.

Stuff the hamburger buns with the vegetables and cheese. Wrap each bun in tin foil and place the buns on the grill or in a 375°F oven until the sandwiches are hot and the cheese has melted, about 5 to 8 minutes.

Hoagies

4 hoagie rolls

2 cups cooked vegetables

$1/4$ to $1/2$ cup ranch dressing

So . . . what else do you do with grilled or steamed vegetables? Try this.

SERVES 4

Stuff the hoagie rolls with the vegetables and wrap them in foil. Heat them in the oven 5 to 10 minutes, until heated through. Drizzle the dressing over the top of the vegetables.

BBQ Eggplant

Eggplant is my all-time favorite item to barbecue. When I'm invited to a cookout in Georgia, I always bring my eggplant along to barbecue.

SERVES 4

Mix the soy sauce and orange juice together to form a marinade. Pour the marinade into an oblong baking dish. Place the eggplant steaks, as I call them, in the marinade, turning them to coat both sides. Allow the eggplant to marinate at room temperature for 30 minutes. Place the eggplant steaks on the grill and cook them about 4 minutes on each side. Have the BBQ sauce in a nonstick pan placed directly on the grill. Dunk the grilled eggplant steaks into the BBQ sauce and return them to the grill for another minute of cooking. As the eggplant steaks are removed from the grill, place them in the BBQ sauce and keep them warm on the grill or in the oven until ready to serve. Serve the eggplant steaks in the warm sauce, either on buns or as the main course.

$1/2$ cup soy sauce

Juice of 2 medium oranges

1 large eggplant, sliced lengthwise or crosswise, $1/4$ inch thick

1 cup BBQ Sauce (your favorite)

Frittata

3 to 4 teaspoons vegetable oil (less if you're using a nonstick pan)

4 large eggs, beaten

2 tablespoons milk

1 small onion, finely chopped

4 whole green onions, finely chopped

1/4 red bell pepper, chopped

1/4 yellow bell pepper, chopped

Salt and freshly ground black pepper to taste

This dish is a mixture of eggs and vegetables, and when prepared on the stove top in a frying pan, it is very similar to an omelet but it is not folded.

SERVES 4

Heat the oil in a frying pan. Combine the eggs and milk. Add the remaining ingredients to the egg mixture. Pour the mixture into the frying pan and work it as you would an omelet, moving the cooked part of the mixture to the center and allowing the uncooked portion to settle around the sides of the pan. When the frittata is no longer runny, invert the frying pan onto a plate and slide the uncooked side of the frittata back into the pan. Cook until the frittata is completely set.

Asparagus-Onion Quiche

This is a great, classic dish. Serve it with a salad, and your meal is complete.

SERVES 6 EASILY

Preheat the oven to 365°F. Roll the dough out and fit it into a 9-inch deep-dish pie pan or quiche baking dish. Sprinkle the Swiss cheese over the dough. In a large skillet, heat the olive oil. Add the onion and sauté for about 4 minutes until tender. Add the asparagus and salt and pepper to the skillet and combine the ingredients well. Remove the skillet from the heat. In a mixing bowl, beat together the eggs and half-and-half and pour the mixture over the cheese in the pie pan. Add the vegetables and bake for 45 to 60 minutes until the quiche is set. Sprinkle the parsley over the top of the quiche the last 10 minutes of baking.

1 recipe Homemade Pie Crust (page 196)

$^1/_2$ cup grated Swiss cheese

1 tablespoon olive oil

$^1/_2$ medium onion, thinly sliced

$^1/_2$ pound fresh asparagus, steamed and cut into bite-sized pieces

Salt and freshly ground black pepper to taste

4 large eggs

$1^1/_2$ cups half-and-half

1 tablespoon chopped fresh parsley

Onion and Pepper Quiche

1 recipe Homemade Pie Crust
(page 196)

1/4 red bell pepper, chopped

1/4 yellow bell pepper,
chopped

1 small onion, chopped

1/2 cup grated Gruyère
cheese

1/2 cup grated American
cheese

1/4 stick (1 ounce) butter

4 large eggs

6 tablespoons milk

3 tablespoons heavy cream

1/2 teaspoon salt

1/4 teaspoon freshly ground
black pepper

The classic French quiche is made with quite a bit of cream. I make mine with little or no cream, since egg dishes with too much cream seem to be difficult for me to digest.

SERVES 6 EASILY

Preheat the oven to 375°F. Prepare the pie dough and roll it out to fit a 9-inch pie pan. The pie crust can be prebaked, but I prefer it unbaked, cooking everything at the same time. Combine the bell peppers and onion and place them in the pie shell. Add the grated cheeses and dollop with the butter. Whip the eggs with the milk and cream and pour over the vegetables and cheese. Season with salt and pepper. Bake for about 45 to 50 minutes until the quiche is firmly set and the mixture is brown on the top. (To avoid burning the edges of the crust, simply cover the rim of the pie crust with tinfoil after it has browned to your satisfaction and continue baking until the quiche is set.)

Swiss Chard Quiche

I love quiche, and it's so easy to make, I don't know why I don't prepare it more often.

SERVES 6 EASILY

Preheat the oven to 375°F. In a saucepan, sauté the Swiss chard, onion, and mushrooms in the olive oil until the vegetables are tender, about 8 minutes. Pour them into the pie shell. In a mixing bowl, beat together the eggs, cream, salt and pepper, bread crumbs, and cheese. Pour over the vegetables and bake for 55 minutes, or until the eggs are set.

Bunch of Swiss chard, chopped

1 medium onion, diced

8 ounces mushrooms of your choice, sliced

2 tablespoons olive oil

1 recipe Homemade Pie Crust (page 196)

6 large eggs

$^1/_2$ cup heavy cream

Salt and freshly ground black pepper to taste

2 tablespoons bread crumbs

$^1/_4$ cup grated Swiss cheese

Onion-Herb Pie

1/2 stick (2 ounces) butter

2 bunches green onions, chopped (both green and white parts)

1 large onion, diced

4 to 6 ounces wild mushrooms, sliced

1/4 cup chopped fresh parsley

2 tablespoons chopped chives

2 tablespoons fresh basil

2/3 cup cooked rice

4 large hard-boiled eggs, chopped

2 recipes Homemade Pie Crust (page 196)

This can be transformed easily into a quiche by adding four eggs beaten with a half a cup of cream to the following mixture before baking. Just increase the baking time by ten minutes.

SERVES 6 EASILY

Preheat the oven to 375°F. In a saucepan, melt the butter. Add both the onions and mushrooms and cook, covered, about 5 minutes. Add the parsley, chives, and basil and cook for another 3 minutes. Add the rice and eggs, stirring well. Pour into one of the pie crusts and top with the other pie crust. Bake 45 minutes.

Wild Mushroom Tart

If you have any leftover tart, chop it up, wrap it in tortillas, heat, and serve covered in salsa. It's a great breakfast dish.

SERVES 6

Preheat the oven to 375°F. In a skillet, sauté the mushrooms and shallots in the margarine. Add the brandy and herbs and cook about 4 minutes. In a bowl, combine the cream, egg, and egg yolks. Fill the pie crust with the cheese, place the mushrooms and shallots on top, and pour the cream and egg mixture over all. Bake for about 30 minutes, or longer if necessary.

3 ounces porcini mushrooms, reconstituted

10 ounces button or cremini mushrooms, sliced

$1/4$ cup shallots, peeled and chopped

$1/2$ stick (4 ounces) margarine

2 tablespoons brandy

2 tablespoons mixed herbs of your choice

$1/3$ cup heavy cream

1 large egg

2 large egg yolks

1 recipe Homemade Pie Crust (page 196)

$2/3$ cup grated Swiss cheese

Veggie Calzone

1 recipe Basic Pizza
Dough (page 11)

¹/₄ cup olive oil

¹/₄ cup chopped broccoli
florets

¹/₄ cup green peas

¹/₄ cup chopped onions

¹/₄ cup chopped garlic

3 asparagus spears, cut into
1-inch pieces

3 to 4 fresh tomatoes,
chopped or diced, or 1
8-ounce can of tomatoes

Salt and freshly ground black
pepper to taste

Calzone are sort of like pizza sandwiches. You simply take the pizza dough and fold it in half on top of the other ingredients. If you're a sandwich lover, you're happy; if you're a pizza lover, you're happy.

SERVES 4

Prepare the pizza dough. Divide the dough into 2 pieces and roll out each piece to an 8-inch round, or to about the size of a dinner plate. Pour the olive oil in a sauté pan and add the broccoli, green peas, onions, garlic, asparagus, tomatoes, and salt and pepper. Sauté until the vegetables are tender, about 10 minutes. Spoon ½ cup of the vegetables in the middle of each round of dough. Fold the dough over and press down, using a bit of water on the edges to make the dough stick. Prick holes in the tops of the calzone and place them on a baking sheet. Bake at 400°F for 10 to 15 minutes, or until the calzone are nicely browned.

Four-Cheese Pizza

There's a little restaurant in Los Angeles that serves an incredible four-cheese pizza on a very thin crust. To get a thin crust pizza, simply slice my basic pizza dough in half and roll it out as thinly as possible. Use less sauce for a thin crust pizza . . . about a quarter of a cup.

SERVES 4 TO 6

Preheat the oven to 400°F. Prepare the pizza dough and roll it out as flat as possible to fit a 14-inch pan. Sprinkle a little cornmeal on the pan before putting the pizza dough on it to help keep the dough from sticking to the pan. Trim the edges if necessary. Spread the sauce on the pizza dough and sprinkle the cheeses on top. Bake for about 10 minutes until the bottom is browned and all the cheese has melted.

1 recipe Basic Pizza Dough (page 11)

2 tablespoons cornmeal

$1/4$ cup My Marinara (page 170)

$1/2$ cup grated American cheese

$1/2$ cup grated Cheddar cheese

$1/2$ cup grated Gruyère cheese

$1/2$ cup grated asiago cheese

Cheeseless Pizza

1 recipe Basic Pizza Dough
 (page 11)

¹/₂ cup My Marinara
 (page 170)

1 cup vegetables of your
 choice, chopped

For those of you who are watching your fat intake, you can make pizza without cheese. I've tried cheeseless pizza in several restaurants, and it's pretty good. You can also use soy cheese as a fairly good substitute.

SERVES 4 TO 6

Preheat the oven to 400°F. Prepare the pizza dough and roll it out to fit a 14-inch pan, trimming the edges if necessary. Spoon the sauce over the dough and top it with the vegetables. Bake until the pizza dough browns on the outside edges. I'm not trying to tempt you, but I thought I'd mention that a little grated cheese sprinkled on top is wonderful.

Garlic and Onion with Tomato Pizza

~~~

This pizza is like having a double marinara pizza, except the second marinara is unmixed. Onions, garlic, and tomatoes on top of thick homemade dough! It is indescribably delicious! Throw a few chopped fresh basil leaves over the top for even more flavor.

SERVES 4 TO 6

Preheat the oven to 400°F. Prepare the pizza dough and roll it out to fit a 14-inch pan, trimming the edges if necessary. Spoon the sauce into the center of the dough, then spread it out with the back of a spoon, leaving a ½- to 1-inch border. Mix together the onion and garlic and sprinkle them over the pizza. Place the tomato slices on top and sprinkle the cheese over the entire pizza. Bake until the cheese melts and the crust browns, about 15 minutes.

1 recipe Basic Pizza Dough (page 11)

½ cup My Marinara (page 170)

1 large onion, diced

5 garlic cloves, diced

2 medium tomatoes, sliced

¾ cup shredded mozzarella cheese

Pizza Primavera

1 recipe Basic Pizza Dough
(page 11)

1 small eggplant, julienned

Bunch of broccoli, stems
removed, florets chopped
into bite-sized pieces

2 tablespoons olive oil

1 cup My Marinara
(page 170)

$^1/_3$ cup carrots, sliced and
steamed

2 ripe tomatoes, sliced

4 artichoke hearts, cut up

3 tablespoons fresh parsley

3 tablespoons fresh basil

1 cup cubed mozzarella
cheese

The vegetables I've used here are some of my favorites. I encourage you to use the vegetables of your choice. I guess I could call this my "salad pizza" because of the combination of wonderful vegetables and rich marinara sauce. When baked, it's like serving your garden on dough.

SERVES 4 TO 6

Preheat the oven to 400°F. Prepare the pizza dough and roll it out to fit a 14-inch pan. In a saucepan, sauté the eggplant and broccoli in the oil for 4 to 6 minutes. Cover the pizza dough with the sauce. Place a layer of eggplant and broccoli on top of the sauce and continue layering with the remainder of the ingredients, ending with the mozzarella cheese. Bake about 15 to 20 minutes until the cheese is melted and bubbly.

Wild Pizza

I call this "wild pizza" because I use wild mushrooms on it. If they are unavailable, you can make a "tame pizza" by using white button mushrooms.

SERVES 4 TO 6

Preheat the oven to 400°F. Prepare the pizza dough and roll it out to fit a 14-inch pan. Spread My Marinara over the dough. In a skillet, sauté the mushrooms in the olive oil. Spread the mushrooms on top of the sauce and cover them with dollops of the roasted garlic. Sprinkle all over with the cheeses and bake until all the cheese melts, about 15 minutes.

1 recipe Basic Pizza Dough (page 11)

$^1/_2$ cup My Marinara (page 170)

10 ounces shiitake mushrooms, chopped

2 tablespoons olive oil

8 garlic cloves, roasted

3 ounces Gruyère cheese, grated

3 ounces Parmesan cheese, grated

3 ounces Swiss cheese, grated

Goat Cheese and Sun-dried Tomatoes Pizza

〰️

1 recipe Basic Pizza Dough (page 11)

1/2 cup sun-dried tomatoes packed in oil

1 tablespoon minced garlic

2 tablespoons dried rosemary

2 tablespoons dried thyme

4 ounces goat cheese

This is a sauceless pizza, reminiscent of focaccia; but it is *a pizza.*

SERVES 4 TO 6

Preheat the oven to 400°F. Prepare the pizza dough and roll it out to fit a 14-inch pan. Place the tomatoes, garlic, rosemary, and thyme on the dough. Crumble the cheese over all and bake until the cheese melts, about 15 minutes.

Feta Cheese Crepes

〰️

1 cup feta cheese

1 cup goat cheese

2 large eggs, beaten

1 tablespoon dried oregano

1 tablespoon chopped fresh dill

1 garlic clove, minced

1/4 teaspoon freshly ground black pepper

3 tablespoons olive oil

8 prepared crepes

For me, there's nothing like crepes for Sunday brunch. They bring back memories of romantic brunches in the Sonoma and Napa valleys when I was a younger man.

SERVES 6

In a medium bowl, mix all the ingredients together except the oil and crepes. Heat the oil in a frying pan over medium-high heat. Fill each crepe with 2 to 4 tablespoons of the cheese mixture. Then to cover it, either fold the crepe in half or place another crepe on top of the cheese mixture. Fry, turning the crepes, until they're soft, about 2 minutes.

Garden Eggs with Salsa

Eggs aren't just for breakfast. This proves they are great at lunch or supper.

SERVES 4

Melt the butter in a skillet and cook the green onions, cilantro, and corn for about 3 minutes. In a bowl, beat together the eggs, milk, and salt. Pour into the skillet and scramble the eggs. Warm the tortillas either in the oven or in a nonstick pan and spread the scrambled eggs on top. Fold the tortillas in half and top them with the cheese and salsa.

1/4 stick (1 ounce) butter

4 whole green onions, chopped

1/4 cup chopped fresh cilantro

1 cup fresh or defrosted frozen corn kernels

4 large eggs, lightly beaten

2 tablespoons milk

Salt to taste

2 large flour tortillas

1/2 cup grated Monterey Jack cheese

1/2 cup Tomato Salsa (page 169)

Egg Salad

3 large hard-boiled eggs, peeled and mashed

1¹/₂ tablespoons mayonnaise

2 teaspoons sweet pickle relish

Salt and freshly ground black pepper to taste

When I was a little boy, my favorite lunch was an egg salad sandwich with Homemade Potato Chips (page 176). Of course, my mama's egg salad was much better than the egg salad I ate at my friends' houses, but I was never known to turn down an egg salad sandwich, no matter who made it.

MAKES ENOUGH FOR 2 SANDWICHES (FOR ME, YOU COULD SERVE 4 SANDWICHES)

In a small mixing bowl, combine the eggs, mayonnaise, and relish. Mix thoroughly and season with the salt and pepper.

My California Egg Salad

Not only does the addition of red bell pepper and ripe olives give basic egg salad a delicious twist, they also add wonderful color.

SERVES 2

Mix all ingredients together in a small mixing bowl.

3 large hard-boiled eggs, peeled and mashed

2 tablespoons mayonnaise

2 teaspoons sweet pickle relish

$^1/_4$ sweet red bell pepper, diced

7 ripe olives, seeded and chopped

Company Egg Salad

One of my favorite ways of serving egg salad, especially to guests, is on a toasted roll with a slice of pan-fried, ripe, red tomato and a slice of American cheese. I serve this open-faced.

SERVES 2

Prepare the egg salad. In a frying pan, heat the oil. Add the tomato slices and fry on both sides for about 40 seconds. Toast the 2 roll halves. On each, place a slice of fried tomato, a slice of cheese, and egg salad.

1 recipe Egg Salad (page 112) or My California Egg Salad (above)

1 teaspoon olive oil

2 thick slices of ripe red tomato

1 hoagie roll, sliced in half

2 slices American cheese

Hearty Main Dishes

Stuffed Eggplant

FOR THE EGGPLANT SHELLS

2 eggplants, sliced in half

4 tablespoons olive oil

4 garlic cloves, minced

Salt and freshly ground black pepper to taste

FOR THE STUFFING

2 tablespoons olive oil plus more if needed

Eggplant pulp

2 yellow onions, diced

4 garlic cloves, minced

1 cup mushrooms, washed and thinly sliced

$^1/_4$ cup sun-dried tomatoes, chopped

$^1/_4$ cup dry white wine

1 tablespoon pine nuts, toasted

$^1/_4$ cup grated Parmesan cheese

$^1/_3$ cup chopped fresh parsley

Eggplant is one of the best vegetables to stuff, and you'll love this stuffing mixture because of the blend of vegetables and nuts. And the sun-dried tomatoes give it a pestolike quality. However, experiment on your own by trying other combinations.

SERVES 4 TO 6

Preheat the oven to 400°F. Scoop the pulp from the eggplant halves and set it aside. In a small bowl, mix the olive oil with the garlic and salt and pepper and baste the inside of the eggplant shells with this mixture. Bake the shells for about 15 minutes. Then remove the shells from the oven and lower the heat to 350°F.

Place the 2 tablespoons olive oil in a sauté pan and sauté the eggplant pulp and onions for about 4 minutes. Add the minced garlic along with the mushrooms and cook another 4 to 5 minutes. Add more oil if needed. Add the tomatoes, wine, and pine nuts and cook until the vegetables are tender. Stuff the eggplant shells with the pulp mixture and top with the Parmesan cheese and parsley. Bake, covered with tinfoil, for 20 to 30 minutes. Remove the tinfoil for the last 5 minutes of baking in order for the eggplant to brown.

Eggplant Parmesan

~~~~~~~~

This is my favorite way to cook eggplant. Preparing the eggplant is the key to the success of this dish. The morning I plan to make eggplant Parmesan, I slice the eggplant a quarter of an inch thick, place it in a bowl, and salt it on all sides. I then refrigerate the eggplant, covered, for at least three hours. The salt extracts the bitterness which is sometimes apparent in eggplant dishes. Then I drain the eggplant, rinse it, and prepare the recipe.

SERVES 4

Preheat the oven to 375°F. Using about 2 tablespoons of the oil, grease a baking dish. Heat the remainder of the oil in a frying pan. Dip the eggplant slices in the beaten egg and then coat them on both sides with the flour. Fry the slices until they are brown. Place the cooked slices on paper towels to absorb any excess oil. In the baking dish, place a layer of eggplant slices, about ¼ cup of My Marinara, half of the Parmesan, and ¼ cup of the mozzarella. Cover with another ¼ cup of the sauce, another layer of eggplant, and top if off with the remaining cheese and sauce. (I usually only make 2 layers.) Bake about 40 minutes. It's great either hot or cold.

¼ to ½ cup oil, for cooking

1 large eggplant, cut into ¼-inch slices and salted

1 to 2 large eggs, beaten

½ cup all-purpose flour

1½ cups My Marinara (page 170)

¾ cup grated Parmesan cheese

½ cup diced mozzarella cheese

Easy Eggplant Parmesan

1 large eggplant, peeled and sliced

$^1/_4$ to $^1/_2$ cup olive oil

2 cups My Marinara (page 170)

$^1/_4$ pound mozzarella cheese

$^1/_4$ teaspoon dried thyme

$^1/_4$ teaspoon dried oregano

$^1/_4$ teaspoon dried basil

$^1/_4$ cup grated Parmesan cheese

Don't confuse easy with quick. Easy means not complicated. Quick means in very little time. In this eggplant Parmesan, I peel the eggplant to help remove the bitterness (since we're not salting or frying it first). This takes some time, but it's a winner.

SERVES 4

Preheat the oven to Broil. Grease a baking dish. Place the eggplant slices on a baking sheet and drizzle them with the oil, coating them well. Broil for 5 to 10 minutes. Remove the eggplant slices from the oven and turn the oven down to 350°F. Place a layer of eggplant slices in the greased baking dish, topped with a layer of My Marinara and mozzarella. Mix the herbs together and sprinkle half of the mixture over the mozzarella. Layer again the eggplant, My Marinara, the remaining herbs, and the Parmesan. Bake for 1 hour.

Portobello Parmesan

~~~~~

I love this mushroom. One day, I decided to substitute mushrooms for the eggplant in my eggplant Parmesan recipe, and it was great . . . and you don't have to worry about salting down the mushrooms as you would the eggplant. The battered and fried portobello is just incredible—earthy but not too strong. When it is smothered with the cheeses and marinara sauce, it just makes you want to sing!

SERVES 4 TO 6

Preheat the oven to 375°F. Heat all but about 2 tablespoons of the oil in a frying pan. Use the remaining 2 tablespoons of oil to grease a baking dish. Dip the mushrooms in the beaten egg and coat them on both.sides with the flour, then fry them until they are brown. Place the cooked mushrooms on a paper towel to absorb the excess oil. In the prepared baking dish, place a layer of the mushrooms, about ¼ cup of My Marinara, half the Parmesan cheese, and half the mozzarella cheese. Cover with another ¼ cup of My Marinara, followed by a layer of mushrooms, the remaining cheeses, and cover the entire dish with the remainder of My Marinara. Bake about 40 minutes.

¼ to ½ cup oil, for cooking

5 portobello mushrooms, sliced in half lengthwise

1 to 2 large eggs, beaten

½ cup all-purpose flour

1½ cups My Marinara (page 170)

¾ cup grated Parmesan cheese

½ cup diced mozzarella cheese

Eggplant Enchiladas

4 medium eggplants, peeled
and thinly sliced

5 tomatoes, peeled and
diced, or 1 24-ounce can
tomatoes, drained and
chopped

1 tablespoon chopped
fresh basil

2 garlic cloves, minced

1 tablespoon tomato paste

Salt and freshly ground black
pepper to taste

1/2 teaspoon sugar

1/2 cup White Gravy
(page 166)

1/2 cup dry white wine

12 large flour tortillas

I've taken a classic enchilada recipe, removed the meat, of course, and substituted eggplant . . . The flavor is outstanding and the texture is rich and almost meatlike. Don't tell your meat-eating guests they're partaking of vegetarian enchiladas, and watch their reaction later.

SERVES 4 TO 6

Preheat the oven to 350°F. Place the eggplant slices on an oiled baking sheet or in a shallow pan and bake or broil until the eggplant is brown. Allow the eggplant slices to cool. Combine the tomatoes, basil, garlic, tomato paste, salt, pepper, and sugar in a saucepan. Add the eggplant. Simmer for about 10 minutes. Meanwhile, in a small saucepan, combine the white gravy with the wine and heat through. Fill the tortillas with the eggplant mixture, then fold them to form enchiladas. Bake for about 20 minutes until the enchiladas are brown. Before serving, cover the enchiladas with the white gravy.

Nut Loaf

For non—meat eaters worried about not getting enough protein, this recipe is for you. The texture is very firm, almost meatlike. The flavor combination, with the nuts, mushrooms, and garlic, is quite intriguing and very good. By the way, this is my substitute for meat loaf, and you can make a nice sandwich out of a slice of this. It's also great with one of my vegetarian gravies (pages 164 to 166).

SERVES 4 TO 6

Preheat the oven to 350°F. In a large saucepan, sauté the onion, garlic, and mushrooms in the butter. Remove from the heat and combine the rice with the mushroom mixture. Add the remaining ingredients and mix well. Press the mixture into a loaf pan and bake for 1 to 1½ hours.

1 medium onion, chopped

2 garlic cloves, minced

$1/2$ cup mushrooms, chopped

1 ounce dried shiitake mushrooms, reconstituted

$1/4$ stick (1 ounce) unsalted butter

1 cup cooked rice

$3/4$ cup walnuts, toasted

$1/2$ cup cashews

$3/4$ cup peanuts

2 large eggs, beaten

2 tablespoons chopped fresh parsley

$1/2$ teaspoon dried thyme

1 teaspoon dried marjoram

1 teaspoon dried sage

1 cup cottage cheese

12 ounces Cheddar cheese, shredded

Tofu Loaf

1 pound tofu

1 cup chopped fresh parsley, divided in half

5 to 6 carrots, grated

1 medium onion, chopped

3/4 cup fresh bread crumbs, not too dry

4 ounces cream cheese, softened

Salt and freshly ground black pepper to taste

Tofu loaf is a wonderful substitute for meat. This is like the nut loaf. I use fewer ingredients with this one because of the strong, distinct flavors of the vegetables. Adding the tofu makes it a hearty, filling main dish that is easy to prepare. You can serve it with any of the veggie gravies (pages 164 to 166).

SERVES 4 TO 6

Preheat the oven to 350°F. Combine all the ingredients except ½ cup of parsley and pour the mixture into a greased loaf pan. Sprinkle the remaining parsley on top. Bake 45 to 50 minutes until firm.

Sherry Tofu

You can serve this versatile dish over rice or as a side dish with your favorite meal.

SERVES 4

Fry the tofu, covered, in 1 tablespoon of the oil until the tofu is brown. Remove from the heat. In a small bowl, mix together the sherry, soy sauce, and cornstarch and pour over the tofu to marinate. Blanch the snow peas for 1 to 2 minutes, then plunge them into cold water to stop them from cooking. Heat the remaining 2 tablespoons of oil in a skillet or wok and stir-fry the green onions and water chestnuts. Add the snow peas and cashews. When the mixture is combined, add the tofu, lemon juice, and pepper and cook 3 to 5 minutes.

1 pound firm tofu, cut into 1-inch pieces

3 tablespoons vegetable oil

2 tablespoons dry sherry

1 tablespoon soy sauce

1 teaspoon cornstarch

2 cups snow peas

2 whole green onions, minced

$1/2$ cup water chestnuts

$1/2$ cup dry-roasted cashews

Juice of $1/2$ lemon

$1/4$ teaspoon freshly ground black pepper

Plenty Polenta

3 cups milk

3 tablespoons (1¹/₂ ounces) butter

1 teaspoon sugar

¹/₂ teaspoon salt

1 cup yellow cornmeal

1 pound tofu, cut into strips

2 garlic cloves, minced

Salt and freshly ground black pepper to taste

2 cups cooked couscous

2 cups shredded Parmesan cheese

2 cups My Marinara (page 170)

¹/₂ pound mozzarella cheese, shredded

I still say it's grits, but everybody else says it's totally different. They are from the same family. They're both made from ground corn and are cooked in a similar fashion. I call it plenty polenta because it makes a lot and it's so filling. Feel free to cut this recipe in half.

SERVES 6 TO 8

In a large saucepan, bring the milk just to a boil. Add 1 tablespoon of the butter, the sugar, salt, and cornmeal. Stir until the mixture thickens and remove from the heat.

In the remaining 2 tablespoons of butter, sauté the tofu until brown. Add the garlic, salt and pepper, and set aside. Place all of the couscous in a greased casserole dish and cover it with the Parmesan cheese. Press the couscous and Parmesan cheese into the dish and top them with the cooked tofu, half of the sauce, and half of the mozzarella. Place the cornmeal mixture on the top and cover with the remaining sauce and mozzarella cheese. Bake for 20 to 30 minutes.

Pasta for One, Maybe Two

Pasta dishes are great ones to have on hand when friends drop by at mealtime. You can stretch a pasta dish simply by cooking more pasta, and the pasta can be refrigerated for up to four days, or even frozen. The mayonnaise is the key in this recipe. It gives the dish flavor and body. Toasted French rolls or even toasted bagels are terrific with this dish.

SERVES 1 OF ME, 2 OF ANYONE ELSE

In a saucepan, sauté the zucchini, onion, pepper, and green onions in the oil for at least 5 minutes. For softer vegetables, sauté up to 8 minutes. Mix in the basil and thyme. Stir in the soy sauce, Worcestershire sauce, and mayonnaise. Add the pasta to the pan and toss lightly to coat.

1 zucchini, diced

1 small onion, diced

1/4 bell pepper (red, yellow, or green), diced

3 whole green onions, diced

3 tablespoons olive oil or vegetable oil

2 tablespoons dried basil

1 tablespoon dried thyme

2 tablespoons soy sauce

2 tablespoons Worcestershire sauce

3 tablespoons mayonnaise

4 to 6 ounces any variety pasta, cooked

Pasta for One, Maybe Two 2

3 tablespoons olive oil

1 small onion, diced

4 garlic cloves, diced

$1/4$ red bell pepper, diced

$1/4$ yellow bell pepper, diced

4 Roma tomatoes, diced

2 tablespoons water

1 tablespoon dried oregano
or 2 tablespoons fresh
oregano

3 tablespoons dried basil or
6 tablespoons fresh basil

Salt and freshly ground black
pepper to taste

4 to 6 ounces cooked pasta

This pasta sauce is thick and flavorful. You can add up to twelve ounces of pasta without hindering the taste, stretching the dish to three servings. Serve this with your favorite bread. San Francisco sourdough is especially good.

SERVES 1 OF ME, 2 OF ANYONE ELSE

Pour the oil in a pan and heat it. Add the onion, garlic, and bell peppers and sauté about 6 minutes, or until they're soft. Add the tomatoes and water to the pan (the water keeps the mixture from sticking to the pan). Simmer, covered, for about 10 minutes. Add the oregano, basil, and salt and pepper. Add the pasta to the pan and toss until it is thoroughly coated with the sauce and heated through. You can even cover the pan and cook it an additional minute or so.

Peppers and Pasta

If you have these ingredients around the house, this recipe can be prepared quickly and easily . . . in fifteen minutes or less. I always make sure I have plenty of fresh vegetables on hand.

SERVES 4

In a large sauté pan, heat the oil and sauté the peppers, tomatoes, onion, garlic, half the basil, the rosemary, and thyme. Cook until the vegetables are tender. Pour this mixture over the pasta and toss to combine well. Sprinkle the finished dish with the remaining basil and Parmesan cheese.

2 tablespoons olive oil

2 red bell peppers, cored and diced or thinly sliced

2 yellow bell peppers, cored and diced or thinly sliced

4 whole tomatoes, chopped, or 1 16-ounce can tomatoes, chopped and drained

1 onion, chopped

2 to 3 garlic cloves, chopped

2 ounces chopped fresh basil, divided in half

1 ounce chopped fresh rosemary

1 ounce chopped fresh thyme

1 pound penne, cooked

1/2 cup shredded Parmesan cheese

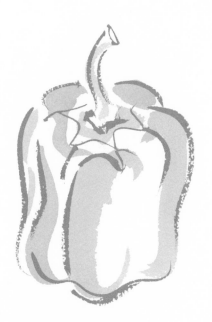

Asparagus with Sun-dried Tomatoes over Pasta

∿∿∿

3 tablespoons extra virgin olive oil

1/2 pound asparagus, cut into 1-inch pieces

1/4 cup sun-dried tomatoes, reconstituted either in olive oil or white wine

1/2 teaspoon dried thyme

2 to 3 tablespoons chopped fresh parsley

Salt and freshly ground black pepper to taste

1/2 to 1 pound pasta of your choice, cooked

1/4 cup grated Parmesan cheese

Sun-dried tomatoes are one of my favorite things, and combined with asparagus, they create a memorable dish.

SERVES 4

Heat the oil in a saucepan and sauté the asparagus for about 4 minutes. Add the tomatoes, thyme, parsley, and salt and pepper. Sauté an additional 3 to 5 minutes. Pour the vegetables over the cooked pasta and sprinkle the Parmesan cheese over the top.

Creamy Artichoke Pasta

Any dish containing cheese, artichokes, and pasta is bound to be good. This one is great.

SERVES 4 TO 6

Place the oil and shallots in a large frying pan and sauté them about 2 minutes. Add the garlic and vermouth and cook another 2 to 3 minutes. Add the artichoke hearts, lemon juice, salt and pepper, dill, thyme, and pimiento to the pan and sauté an additional 6 to 7 minutes until the liquid has reduced a bit. Add the cottage cheese and ricotta cheese. Heat through, then pour the mixture over the cooked penne. Sprinkle with the grated asiago cheese.

2 to 3 tablespoons olive oil

2 shallots, minced

2 garlic cloves, minced

$1/2$ cup vermouth

8 fresh artichoke hearts, steamed and diced, or 1 12-ounce can artichoke hearts, drained and diced

2 tablespoons freshly squeezed lemon juice

Salt and freshly ground black pepper to taste

1 tablespoon minced fresh dill

2 teaspoons fresh thyme or $1/2$ teaspoon dried thyme

2 tablespoons slivered pimiento pepper

$1^{1}/2$ cups cottage cheese

$1/2$ cup ricotta cheese

1 pound penne, cooked

$1/4$ cup grated asiago cheese, Parmesan cheese, or Romano cheese

Pasta with Roasted Garlic Sauce

～～～～

2 garlic bulbs

2 tablespoons extra virgin olive oil

1 small onion, sliced

3 8-ounce cans tomatoes with their juice

1/4 cup dry sherry

1 bay leaf

1 pound linguine, cooked

The first time I ate roasted garlic was in the late eighties at the Hilltop Cafe in Novato, California. You can make the best and easiest garlic bread by just spreading roasted garlic on toast.

SERVES 6 TO 8

Preheat the oven to 400°F. Brush the garlic bulbs with the olive oil and bake them for about 30 minutes. After the garlic has cooled, squeeze the pulp out and make a paste. Meanwhile, cook the onion and tomatoes with their juice in a saucepan for about 10 minutes. Stir in the sherry and bay leaf. Add the garlic paste and cook until the sauce thickens. Remove the bay leaf and serve over the linguine.

Pasta with Cauliflower

This recipe is easy and quick. Any vegetable will do . . . broccoli, cabbage . . . and the same is true with the pasta. I'm using penne, but you might prefer linguine.

SERVES 4 TO 6

Heat the butter and oil in a large sauté pan or frying pan and sauté the cauliflower for 6 to 8 minutes. Add the onion, carrot, garlic, tomatoes, basil, oregano, rosemary, and salt and pepper. Heat through and serve over the penne.

$^1/_4$ stick (1 ounce) butter

2 tablespoons olive oil

Head of cauliflower, trimmed of stems and cut into small florets

1 onion, peeled and chopped

1 carrot, peeled and chopped

3 garlic cloves, peeled and minced

1 32-ounce can plum tomatoes

1 teaspoon dried basil

1 teaspoon dried oregano

1 teaspoon dried rosemary

Salt and freshly ground black pepper to taste

1 pound penne, cooked

Spaghetti Gorgonzola

5 whole green onions, minced

2 garlic cloves, peeled and minced

$^1/_2$ pound snow peas

2 tablespoons dried coriander

1 tablespoon olive oil

$^1/_4$ cup dry white wine

1 pound spaghetti, cooked

Salt and freshly ground black pepper to taste

4 ounces Gorgonzola cheese, crumbled, for garnish

Gorgonzola is a wonderful cheese. If you don't have any on hand, just use any cheese you like.

SERVES 4 TO 6

Sauté the green onions, garlic, snow peas, and coriander in the olive oil and white wine for 5 to 6 minutes. Pour the spaghetti into the vegetable mixture and combine. Season with salt and pepper. Top with the Gorgonzola cheese and serve.

Spaghetti and Walnut Sauce

This recipe goes a long way. Spaghetti, walnuts, and ricotta cheese work beautifully in this sauce.

SERVES 4

Place the nuts and water in a food processor and process until a paste is formed. Sauté the garlic in the olive oil. Add the nut paste and stir quickly to combine, adding more oil if needed. Add the cheese, parsley, and spaghetti. Toss and serve.

1/2 pound mixed nuts

2 tablespoons water

3 garlic cloves, peeled

2 tablespoons olive oil, plus more if needed

1/4 cup ricotta cheese

1/4 cup minced fresh parsley

1 pound spaghetti, cooked

Mushroom Fettuccine

This is easy. You start by sautéing portobello, cremini, and shiitake mushrooms in butter. Add cream, dry sherry, and chives . . . you get the picture. You've got a great-tasting pasta.

SERVES 4 TO 6

In a saucepan, sauté the onion and mushrooms in the butter. Add the cream, sherry, and chives. Cook until the liquid reduces and thickens. Pour the fettuccine on top, toss, and serve.

1 large onion, chopped

1 1/2 pounds mixed mushrooms (portobello, cremini, shiitake), chopped

3 tablespoons (1 1/2 ounces) butter

1 1/4 cups heavy cream

2 tablespoons dry sherry

1 tablespoon fresh chives

1 pound fettuccine or your favorite pasta, cooked

Potatoes Like Lasagna

2 large potatoes, peeled and sliced lengthwise

2 cups My Marinara (page 170)

2 large eggs

15 ounces ricotta cheese

$^1/_2$ cup grated Parmesan cheese

$^1/_2$ teaspoon salt

$^1/_4$ teaspoon freshly ground black pepper

1 pound mozzarella cheese, sliced

As much as I love pasta, sometimes I feel pasta'd out. That doesn't happen often, I must admit, but when it does, this dish soothes my pasta overload. This has a flavor similar to that of lasagna, but the texture is softer because of the potatoes.

SERVES 4

Preheat the oven to 375°F and grease and flour a 13 × 9-inch baking dish. Place a layer of potato slices on the bottom of the dish and cover it with approximately $^1/_4$ cup of sauce. In a mixing bowl, beat the eggs with the ricotta and Parmesan cheeses and salt and pepper. Pour about half of the cheese mixture on top of the potatoes and sauce and place a layer of mozzarella on top of that. Continue layering the potatoes, sauce, cheese mixture, and mozzarella until all the ingredients are used up—you should end with a top layer of mozzarella cheese. Bake for about 45 to 50 minutes. The bottom layer of potatoes will be soft and the top layer will be a bit firmer. If you prefer a softer top layer, bake an additional 15 to 20 minutes, or cover during the initial baking, uncovering the last 10 minutes to brown the top.

Rainbow Lasagna

~~~~~

While writing this book, I was asked to make a guest
appearance on the popular, award-winning PBS show Reading
Rainbow, hosted by Levar Burton. Needless to say, I was thrilled.
I have enjoyed his work since his powerful performance in
Alex Haley's Roots.

The day I spent with Levar, his wife, Stephanie, and the rest of
the production team was wonderful. We did a show on the science of
cooking. One of the things Levar and I talked about was how food
expands and shrinks. Rice is a good example of a food that expands
during cooking—it nearly triples in size when cooked in water.
Spinach, on the other hand, shrinks. Twelve cups of uncooked spinach
cooks down to just two cups. To prove the point, I prepared a lasagna-
type dish on the show using rice and spinach instead of the traditional
ingredients of noodles, ricotta cheese, and eggs. Here's my recipe in
honor of Reading Rainbow.

1 teaspoon oil

4 cups cooked rice

2 cups My Marinara
(page 170)

1 cup grated mozzarella
cheese or Swiss cheese

2 cups cooked spinach

SERVES 4 TO 6

Preheat the oven to 400°F. Grease a baking dish with the
oil. Spread 2 cups of rice on the bottom of the dish, followed
by about ½ cup of sauce, half of the cheese, and all of the
spinach. Add another ½ cup of sauce and the remainder of
the rice. Then pour the last cup of sauce over the rice and top
with the remaining cheese. Bake at 400°F for the first 15 minutes, then reduce the heat to 350°F and continue baking
another 20 to 25 minutes.

Pesto Lasagna

1 pound ricotta cheese

1/2 cup grated Parmesan cheese

1 cup grated mozzarella cheese

1/4 cup minced fresh parsley

1/4 cup minced whole green onion

2 large eggs

1/2 teaspoon dried marjoram

2 teaspoons minced fresh basil

1/4 teaspoon dried oregano

1/2 teaspoon minced garlic

Salt and freshly ground black pepper to taste

6 cooked lasagna noodles

1 cup My Marinara (page 170)

1 cup pesto

This recipe combines two Italian classics: pesto and lasagna. Remember, you can never use too much garlic.

SERVES 4

Preheat the oven to 375°F. In a bowl, mix together the cheeses, parsley, green onion, and eggs. Add the marjoram, basil, oregano, garlic, and salt and pepper. Place 3 of the noodles in the bottom of a greased baking dish. Cover the noodles with about 1/4 cup of sauce, the cheese mixture, and the pesto. Top with the last 3 noodles, and pour the remaining sauce over the top. Bake for 50 to 60 minutes.

Tofu Lasagna

In addition to being a great food stretcher, tofu can be prepared as and for itself in many different ways: fried, barbecued, and baked. Here I've added crumbled tofu instead of traditional meat to a lasagna recipe, which keeps it hearty and filling yet does not have the animal fat. I think the flavor is outstanding.

SERVES 4

Preheat the oven to 375°F. Grease a baking dish and set it aside. In a saucepan, sauté the onion, mushrooms, and garlic in the oil. In a bowl, mix together the tofu, cheese, eggs, parsley, and salt and pepper. Place 3 of the noodles in the bottom of the baking dish, layer on ¼ cup of the sauce, the mushroom mixture, and the tofu mixture. Spread another ¼ cup of the sauce over the top and place the remaining 3 noodles over that. Cover with the remaining sauce. Bake for 50 to 60 minutes.

1 medium onion, chopped

6 ounces mushrooms, chopped

1 garlic clove, minced

1 tablespoon vegetable oil

1 pound firm tofu, mashed or crumbled

¹/₂ cup grated Romano cheese or other Italian cheese

2 large eggs, beaten

¹/₄ cup chopped fresh parsley

Salt and freshly ground black pepper to taste

6 cooked lasagna noodles

1 cup My Marinara (page 170)

Spicy Couscous

1 cup diced yellow squash

1 cup broccoli or cauliflower florets

$1/2$ cup diced red onion

1 garlic clove, chopped

1 cup garbanzo beans

2 tablespoons olive oil

$1/2$ teaspoon ground cumin

$1/2$ teaspoon curry powder

$1/2$ teaspoon paprika

$1/2$ teaspoon red pepper flakes (optional)

Salt and freshly ground black pepper to taste

2 cups apple juice

3 cups couscous

Parsley, for garnish

Couscous is a wonderful Mediterranean granular pasta that cooks quickly and mixes well with other foods and absorbs the flavors that it's cooked with. If you try it, you're sure to become a big fan. When combined with the array of flavors in this recipe, it's sure to please everyone in your family.

SERVES 4 TO 6

In a large skillet, sauté the squash, broccoli, onions, garlic, and garbanzo beans in the olive oil for 8 to 10 minutes, adding more oil if needed. Add the cumin, curry powder, paprika, red pepper flakes, and salt and pepper. Turn the heat down and simmer for 4 to 5 minutes. In a saucepan, bring the apple juice to a boil and add the couscous. Remove the saucepan from the heat and let it sit until the couscous absorbs all the liquid, about 10 to 15 minutes. Mix the couscous with the sautéed vegetables and garnish with parsley.

Tabbouleh

I got my first tabbouleh recipe from Mary Ayub in San Diego, California. Nowadays, I just call it "parsley salad." Serve it like a salad or stuffed in pita bread.

SERVES 4

Soften the bulgur in a cup of warm water until it swells and is soft. Drain any water that isn't absorbed.

Mix all the ingredients together.

Note: If you don't want to presoften the bulgur, mix the tabbouleh at least one day ahead before serving; then the bulgur will absorb the juices of the other ingredients and become softened.

$3/4$ cup bulgur, softened

3-pound bunch of parsley, finely chopped

Bunch of mint, finely chopped

5 ripe tomatoes, diced

Juice of 1 lemon

$1/2$ cup olive oil

Salt and freshly ground black pepper to taste

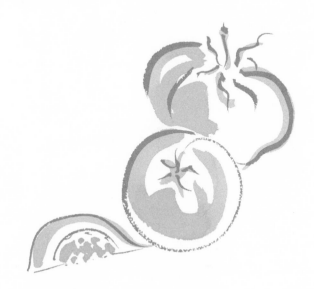

Apple-Squash Casserole

2 medium butternut squashes, peeled, cored, sliced, and steamed

$^1/_2$ stick (2 ounces) butter, divided

$^1/_4$ cup plus 2 teaspoons light brown sugar

$^1/_4$ teaspoon ground nutmeg

1 teaspoon ground cinnamon

1 teaspoon salt

2 Rome Beauty apples, peeled, cored, and diced

2 cups cornflakes, crushed

$^1/_2$ cup chopped pecans

This is excellent as a luncheon casserole or a wonderful side dish for supper. You can even make it a dessert simply by adding $^1/_4$ cup more sugar.

SERVES 4

Preheat the oven to 350°F. Mash the squash together with 2 tablespoons of the butter, the ¼ cup of the brown sugar, the nutmeg, cinnamon, and salt. Pour the mixture into a greased baking dish and cover with the apples. Melt the remaining 2 tablespoons of butter. Mix together the cornflakes, pecans, and the 2 teaspoons of brown sugar with the butter. Layer this mixture over the top of the apples. Bake for about 15 to 20 minutes, or until the top is nicely browned.

Pasta Casserole

I absolutely love this recipe. It's as much fun to make as it is to eat. I usually make this with my son Curtis Jr., who sits on the countertop adjacent to the sink so he can "help." His idea of helping is to eat the spiral noodles (and handfuls of cheese) while I'm doing all the chopping. Just remember to take your time making the cheese sauce; you don't want to burn it.

SERVES 4 TO 6

Preheat the oven to 375°F. Place the pasta in a buttered 3-quart casserole dish. Mix together the cream, wine, and pepper sauce in a heavy saucepan and gradually add the cheeses until they are melted. Whisk this mixture until it is smooth. Place the olive oil in a sauté pan and sauté the spinach and onion, covered, until the onion is tender and the spinach cooks down, about 10 minutes. Add the sage, thyme, parsley, and salt and pepper, blending them in well. Layer the spinach onion mixture over the pasta, followed by the cheese mixture. Cover the top with the sliced tomatoes and nuts. Bake for 30 minutes.

1 pound spiral pasta, cooked

1 cup heavy cream

$1/2$ cup dry white wine

Dash of pepper sauce (optional)

3 cups cubed Cheddar cheese

1 cup crumbled blue cheese

1 cup chopped Brie cheese

$1/2$ cup freshly ground Parmesan cheese

1 tablespoon olive oil

5 to 6 ounces fresh spinach, washed well

1 medium onion, chopped

$1^1/2$ teaspoons dried sage

1 teaspoon dried thyme

2 tablespoons chopped fresh parsley

Salt and freshly ground black pepper to taste

3 ripe tomatoes, thinly sliced

$1/2$ cup nuts, such as hazelnuts

Chili Casserole

1 cup sour cream or
plain yogurt

2 3-ounce cans red or green
chiles, chopped

2 jalapeño peppers, diced
(optional)

5 8-ounce cans tomatillos

1/3 cup diced mushrooms

3 whole green onions,
chopped

1 tablespoon butter

1 tablespoon finely chopped
fresh cilantro

Salt and freshly ground black
pepper to taste

3 cups cooked yellow rice

1/2 pound Monterey Jack
cheese, sliced into 1/2-inch
strips

1/2 cup grated sharp Cheddar
cheese

This dish packs a wallop from the chiles, jalapeño peppers, and those wonderful green Mexican tomatillos added to the sour cream (or yogurt). I call the combination my "South of the Border" sour cream.

SERVES 4

Preheat the oven to 350°F and butter a casserole dish. In a mixing bowl, combine the sour cream, chiles, jalapeños, and tomatillos and set aside. In a small pan, sauté the mushrooms and green onions in the butter for about 4 minutes. Add the cilantro and salt and pepper, stirring well to mix. Combine the mushroom mixture with the sour cream mixture. Place a layer of the rice in the casserole dish, and then a layer of the sour cream mixture, continuing until all ingredients are used up, ending with a layer of rice. Place the strips of Monterey Jack cheese over the rice and sprinkle with the Cheddar cheese. Bake for 20 to 30 minutes.

Cauliflower-Cheese Casserole

～～～～

Cauliflower is one of the most versatile vegetables. You can do just about anything with it, cooked or raw. This casserole is particularly good, so try it even if you don't have cauliflower readily available to you. Just substitute any other fresh vegetable.

SERVES 4

Preheat the oven to 375°F and butter a casserole dish. In a sauté pan, sauté the garlic in the oil over medium heat, taking care not to burn the garlic. Add the tomatoes and mix. Stir in the cauliflower and toss well. Pour a bit of water in the pan, cover the pan, and cook for about 10 minutes, or until the cauliflower is tender. Meanwhile, in a bowl, mix together the eggs, ricotta and Parmesan cheeses, parsley, nutmeg, pepper flakes, salt and pepper, and Muenster cheese. Combine this mixture with the cauliflower mixture, add the milk, and spoon into the buttered casserole dish. Sprinkle the top with the nuts and bake 25 minutes, or until the casserole is brown.

2 garlic cloves, minced

2 tablespoons olive oil

$1/2$ cup diced tomatoes

Medium head of cauliflower, cut into small florets

$1/4$ cup water

3 large eggs

1 cup ricotta cheese

$1/4$ cup shredded Parmesan cheese

2 tablespoons minced fresh parsley

$1/2$ teaspoon ground nutmeg

1 teaspoon hot or red pepper flakes (optional)

Salt and freshly ground black pepper to taste

$1/4$ to $1/2$ cup grated Muenster cheese

$1/2$ cup milk

$1/4$ to $1/2$ cup any variety of nuts, toasted

Chilereno Casserole

~~~~

4 large eggs

1 1/2 cups milk

2 tablespoons all-purpose flour

Salt and freshly ground black pepper to taste

3 7-ounce cans whole green chiles

4 cups shredded Monterey Jack cheese

The first time I ever had chiles rellenos was in San Jose, California, compliments of Chef Tom Lyon. Tom's not really a chef, he's just a really dear friend who loves to cook Mexican food and does a great job of it. His chiles rellenos are fried and rather crispy. The taste is outstanding. My baked version loses none of the flavor of the melted Monterey Jack cheese along with the egg floured batter of the rellenos, but it does have fewer calories. This is my baked version.

SERVES 4

Preheat the oven to 350°F. Spray an oblong baking dish with vegetable oil spray. In a bowl, combine the eggs, milk, flour, and salt and pepper and whisk together. Arrange a layer of the chiles alternately with a layer of the cheese in the baking dish until both are used up. Pour the egg mixture over all and bake about 1 hour and 15 minutes. Cool before serving.

Baked Rigatoni

I'm using rigatoni here, but any spiral pasta will do. Just remember that when it comes to pasta, always use your favorite. The flavor mixture of eggplant, pepper, fresh herbs, and cheese here is incredible. This dish can be served hot or cold, but personally, my favorite way is hot.

SERVES 4 TO 5

Preheat the oven to 400°F. In a large roasting pan or casserole dish, place the slices of eggplant, layered with the mushrooms, peppers, and onion. Drizzle the olive oil over the top, season with salt and pepper, and roast until the vegetables and peppers are tender, about 45 minutes. When they are cooked, cover them with the rigatoni and top that with the sauce, basil, and cheeses. Bake for about 20 to 30 minutes.

8 medium Japanese eggplants, sliced

1 pound mushrooms, washed and quartered

2 red bell peppers, julienned

1 medium onion, minced

2 tablespoons olive oil

Salt and freshly ground black pepper to taste

1 pound rigatoni, cooked

3 cups My Marinara (page 170)

3 tablespoons chopped fresh basil

1/2 pound provolone cheese, sliced

1/2 pound Parmesan cheese, grated

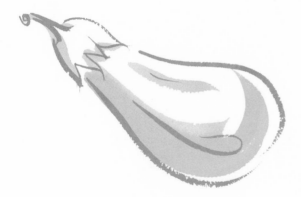

Tomato and Pasta Casserole

1/4 stick (1 ounce) butter

1 garlic clove, minced

1 onion, chopped

1 red bell pepper, sliced

1 yellow bell pepper, sliced

1 green bell pepper, sliced

1 16-ounce can plum
tomatoes

2 tablespoons tomato paste

Salt and freshly ground black
pepper to taste

1/2 pound macaroni, cooked

10 ounces spinach, cooked

4 ounces mozzarella
cheese, grated

This dish is a great entrée or side dish. You can easily make a double recipe and freeze half for later. If fresh spinach is unavailable, you can always use frozen or canned. Just make sure to squeeze out all the excess water before adding it to the dish.

SERVES 4

Preheat the oven to 350°F. Grease a casserole dish and set it aside. In a saucepan, melt the butter and add the garlic, onion, peppers, plum tomatoes, tomato paste, and salt and pepper. Cover and cook about 10 minutes. In the casserole dish, layer the macaroni, the spinach, and the tomato mixture and cover with the mozzarella. Bake for 20 to 30 minutes.

Vegetable Paella

Not only is paella the name of the food, but it is also the name of the vessel in which the food is prepared. In lieu of a paella pan, a frying pan or Dutch oven will do.

SERVES 4

In a large pot, in the oil, sauté the onions, garlic, and bell peppers for about 5 minutes. Add the tomatoes, rice, 1 cup of the stock, and the white wine. Cook slowly, uncovered, over medium heat until the liquid is mostly absorbed. Add the remaining 3 cups of stock, saffron, green beans, garbanzo beans, peas, olives, paprika, and salt and pepper. Cook for 20 to 30 minutes.

2 tablespoons olive oil

2 onions, chopped

5 garlic cloves, crushed

1 red bell pepper, julienned

1 green bell pepper, julienned

4 ripe tomatoes, peeled and chopped

2 cups long grain rice

4 cups vegetable stock (page 20)

$1/2$ cup dry white wine

1 teaspoon saffron threads

$1/2$ cup green beans, cut into $1/2$-inch pieces

2 16-ounce cans garbanzo beans, drained

1 cup frozen peas

$1/2$ cup black olives

1 teaspoon paprika

Salt and freshly ground black pepper to taste

Easy Mushroom Vegetable Paella

1/2 pound snow peas,
cut diagonally

1/2 pound wild mushrooms,
sliced

1/2 pound tofu, fried
and cut up

1/8 teaspoon ground
saffron

3 tablespoons oil

2 cups long grain rice

3/4 cup vegetable stock
(page 20)

If you can't find saffron, just leave it out. Though saffron adds a wonderful color, the dish becomes much less expensive to prepare without it. Turmeric is a good substitute for saffron. Paella gets its name from the type of pan it was originally cooked in. The paella pan looks very much like a large pie pan with its flat bottom and shallow, sloping sides. Don't worry, though, if you don't have a paella pan, you can use whatever pot you have on hand.

SERVES 4

In a large saucepan, sauté the snow peas, mushrooms, tofu, and saffron in the oil for 5 minutes. Add the rice and stir until it is well coated with the oil. Add the stock, stirring well, cover, and simmer for 15 to 20 minutes, or until the rice is cooked.

Rice Primavera

If you love rice, and you love vegetables, this is your dish. This dish not only tastes great, it looks good too. This easy main (or side) dish will probably become something you will want to prepare once or twice a week. It's great hot, but can also be served cold.

SERVES 4

In a large saucepan, cook the onion, garlic, pepper, and potatoes in the oil for 8 minutes, or until the pepper and vegetables are tender. Add the stock and the rest of the vegetables and season with salt and pepper. Simmer for about 10 to 15 minutes. Add the rice, cover, and cook until most of the liquid is absorbed, about 30 minutes, and the rice is cooked.

1 large onion, diced

3 large garlic cloves, crushed

1 red bell pepper, julienned

$^1/_2$ pound small red potatoes, quartered

$^1/_4$ cup olive oil

5 cups vegetable stock (page 20)

1 16-ounce can tomatoes, drained

1 pound fresh green beans, cut into 1-inch strips

1 8-ounce can artichoke hearts, quartered

$^1/_2$ pound fresh or defrosted frozen lima beans

$^1/_2$ pound fresh asparagus

Salt and freshly ground black pepper to taste

2 cups long grain white rice

Vegetable Main Dishes

Asparagus with Black Bean Sauce

~~~~~~~~

1/4 cup vegetable stock (page 20)

1 teaspoon sugar

1 tablespoon dark sesame oil

2 tablespoons olive oil

1/2 medium onion, sliced into slivers

3 garlic cloves, minced

2 pounds fresh asparagus, trimmed and cut into 1-inch pieces

2 8-ounce cans preserved black beans, drained and rinsed

Salt and freshly ground black pepper to taste

1/2 teaspoon crushed red pepper flakes or 1 teaspoon chili sauce

1 teaspoon cornstarch dissolved in 2 tablespoons water

This dish is an easy stir-fry using my son Curtis Jr.'s favorite vegetable: asparagus. The olive oil and dark sesame make a neat flavor combination that blends well with the black bean and asparagus.

SERVES 4

In a small bowl, combine the stock, sugar, and sesame oil to make a tamari sauce and set it aside. Heat a wok over high heat and put in the olive oil. Stir-fry the onion and garlic for about 30 seconds. Add the asparagus, black beans, salt and pepper, and red pepper flakes and toss, cooking until asparagus pieces are tender, about 3 to 4 minutes. Add the cornstarch to the wok and cook until thickened. Pour over rice and serve with the tamari sauce.

Bok Choy-Shiitake Stir-Fry

Bok choy is a member of the cabbage family and is found in many Asian dishes. Once you try bok choy, you'll want to use it in your traditional American dishes because the flavor is so outstanding (sweet, but be careful not to overcook it). And the texture is nice and crunchy.

SERVES 4

In a large skillet, sauté the mushrooms in the oil for 3 to 5 minutes. Add the garlic, ginger, bok choy, peppers, green onions, sesame oil, sherry, soy sauce, and salt. Stir-fry until the bok choy and peppers are tender, about 5 to 8 minutes. Add the noodles and mix. Serve on a platter and sprinkle the top with the sesame seeds.

$1/2$ pound shiitake mushrooms, washed and sliced

2 tablespoons vegetable oil

3 garlic cloves, minced

1 tablespoon grated fresh ginger

Head of bok choy, chopped into 1-inch or smaller pieces

$1/4$ cup chopped red bell peppers

Bunch green onions, chopped (both green and white parts)

1 tablespoon dark sesame oil

2 tablespoons sweet sherry

2 tablespoons soy sauce

Salt to taste

8 to 12 ounces Oriental noodles, cooked

2 tablespoons sesame seeds, for garnish

Pepper and Veggie Stir-Fry

~~~

1/4 cup peanut oil

1/2 pound tofu, diced into
  1-inch cubes

2 garlic cloves, chopped

2 green bell peppers,
  cored and julienned

2 red bell peppers,
  cored and julienned

4 whole green onions,
  chopped

2 large ripe tomatoes,
  chopped

1/4 pound mushrooms,
  washed and thinly sliced

2 tablespoons fresh oregano

Salt and freshly ground black
  pepper to taste

Here's another easy one-dish meal using a common vegetable that is often overlooked . . . the bell pepper. A bell pepper is loaded with vitamins A, B, and C and tastes wonderful. Serve this dish over rice or pasta.

SERVES 3 TO 4

Heat the peanut oil in a frying pan and add the tofu and garlic. Cook 2 to 3 minutes. Add the bell peppers and green onions and cook 3 to 4 minutes longer. Add the remaining ingredients, and stir-fry the mixture another 4 minutes.

Broccoli Stir-Fry with Homemade Oyster Sauce

~~~~~

The wild mushrooms make this dish special because of their strong, distinct, earthy flavors, which are not found in common button mushrooms. I use oyster mushrooms, but you can substitute your favorite variety.

SERVES 5 TO 6

In a skillet, sauté the mushrooms in the oil. In a small bowl, combine the vinegar, soy sauce, and cornstarch and mix well. Remove the mushrooms from the heat, pour the sauce over the mushrooms, and stir to mix.

In a medium frying pan, sauté the broccoli and garlic in the oil for 3 to 5 minutes. Add the onions, red pepper, and tofu and stir-fry until done, about 8 minutes, or if you like them softer, about 10 minutes. Add more oil if needed or place a lid on the frying pan to retain the moisture inside it. Combine the stir-fry mixture with the mushroom sauce and toss thoroughly. Serve over noodles.

FOR THE OYSTER SAUCE

7 oyster mushrooms, washed and finely chopped

3 tablespoons oil

2 ounces rice wine vinegar

10 ounces soy sauce

1 teaspoon cornstarch

FOR THE STIR-FRY

1 pound broccoli, rinsed, stems removed, cut into bite-sized florets

2 garlic cloves, minced

1 tablespoon vegetable oil

$1/2$ cup pearl onions, peeled (if using defrosted frozen onions, drain them)

$1/4$ cup diced red bell pepper

$1/2$ pound tofu, diced into 1-inch pieces

1 recipe Oyster Sauce

Rice Stir-Fry

1 tablespoon vegetable oil

1 tablespoon minced garlic

1 tablespoon minced fresh ginger

1 cup sliced sweet onion

$^1/_2$ head bok choy, chopped

1 cup green peas, fresh or frozen

2 large eggs, beaten

$^1/_2$ pound cooked tofu

2 whole green onions, chopped

$^1/_4$ cup tamari sauce

$^1/_4$ cup dry sherry

$^1/_4$ cup vegetable stock (page 20)

3 cups cooked long grain rice

This is a huge recipe, so if you don't have a wok, use the biggest frying pan or pot you have. This recipe can easily be halved. I think it's special because it's so easy to make, and if unexpected company drops by, you can whip it up in no time and it can be a side dish or the main meal. If you don't have tamari, just use soy sauce.

SERVES 6

In a wok, heat the oil and stir-fry the garlic, ginger, and onion slices until the onion slices are translucent. Add the remaining ingredients and sauté until the eggs are cooked and all the vegetables are heated thoroughly, including the rice.

Vegetable Curry 1

~~~~~

Curry powder is simply a blend of spices, and it's easy to make your own. After preparing this dish, if you find it a bit too hot, next time cut back on the cayenne. To tame the heat in this dish, add a bit of sugar or honey.

SERVES 4

To make the curry powder, combine the cumin seeds, salt, mustard, turmeric, coriander, and cayenne. Grind this mixture together in a coffee grinder.

Heat the butter in a pan and add all the curry powder, stirring to blend. Add the beans, potatoes, carrots, and onion, cover, and cook until the vegetables are tender, about 10 to 15 minutes. Add the yogurt and peas to the pan and stir until all the vegetables are coated with the yogurt and thoroughly heated. Serve over rice.

2 teaspoons cumin seeds

1 teaspoon salt

1 teaspoon ground mustard

2 teaspoons ground turmeric

$^1/_2$ teaspoon ground coriander

$^1/_2$ teaspoon ground cayenne pepper

$^1/_2$ stick (2 ounces) butter

2 cups wax beans or green beans, cut into 1-inch pieces

2 medium red potatoes, peeled and diced

2 medium carrots, peeled and diced

1 red onion, diced

1 cup plain yogurt

1 cup fresh green peas

Vegetable Curry 2

1/2 stick (2 ounces) butter

1/2 teaspoon ground ginger

1/2 teaspoon ground turmeric

1/2 teaspoon ground cayenne pepper

1/2 teaspoon ground coriander

2 pounds vegetables, diced and steamed (use your favorites)

1/2 teaspoon ground cinnamon

2 garlic cloves, crushed

1/2 cup water

3 tablespoons chopped fresh coriander

2 tomatoes, diced

In this curry powder mixture, I've added ground ginger and cinnamon, which gives it a bit of an island flavor. I truly enjoy this particular curry, and I hope you do as well.

SERVES 4

Heat the butter in a large frying pan and add the ginger, turmeric, cayenne, and ground coriander to make a curry powder. Put the steamed vegetables in the frying pan and toss them in the spices. Add the cinnamon, garlic, water, chopped coriander, and tomatoes. Cook for 10 to 15 minutes. Serve over noodles.

Mediterranean Cauliflower

This dish makes me think of my visit to a little town on the Mediterranean named Spilanga. I ate something very similar to this there and the flavor was incredible, so I've tried to re-create it here.

SERVES 4

Preheat the oven to 375°F and butter a casserole or baking dish. In a skillet sauté the cauliflower, garlic, bell pepper, and capers in the olive oil until the vegetables and bell pepper are tender, about 5 to 8 minutes. Season with salt and pepper. Pour the cauliflower mixture into the prepared casserole dish. Top with the bread crumbs, butter, and cheese. Bake for about 10 to 15 minutes until the cheese is bubbly.

2 small heads cauliflower, cut into florets

3 garlic cloves, minced

1 red bell pepper or yellow bell pepper, cored, seeded, and chopped

$^1/_2$ cup capers

2 tablespoons olive oil

Salt and freshly ground black pepper to taste

$^1/_4$ cup seasoned bread crumbs

$^1/_4$ stick (1 ounce) butter, melted

$^1/_4$ cup shredded cheese of your choice

Friday Surprise

2 carrots, sliced

1 cup chopped onion

3 garlic cloves, crushed

4 celery stalks, chopped

1 green bell pepper, seeded
  and diced

1 large tomato, chopped

5 yellow crookneck squashes
  or zucchini, sliced

$^1/_2$ cup corn kernels, fresh,
  defrosted frozen, or canned

$^1/_4$ stick (1 ounce) butter

$^1/_2$ cup vegetable stock
  (page 20)

$^1/_2$ cup cooked pinto beans

$^3/_4$ cup cooked long
  grain rice

1 teaspoon ground cumin

1 teaspoon dried thyme

1 tablespoon chili powder

Salt and freshly ground black
  pepper to taste

$^1/_2$ cup chopped walnuts or
  pecans, for garnish

$^1/_2$ cup shredded Gruyère
  cheese, for garnish

It's Friday, and there's nothing in the refrigerator but leftovers . . . some rice, a few beans, and a little bit of everything in the vegetable bin. Here's a meal.

SERVES 4

Place the carrots, onion, garlic, celery, bell pepper, tomato, squash, and corn into a large pot and sauté in the butter until the vegetables are tender, about 5 minutes. Add the stock, beans, rice, cumin, thyme, chili powder, and salt and pepper. Cook another 30 minutes. Serve in bowls and sprinkle with the nuts and cheese.

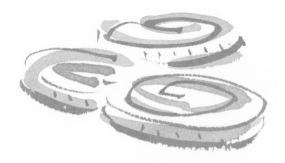

Veggie-Cabbage Rolls

This recipe is great fun to make as long as you remember the most important ingredient . . . patience. Get the kids involved. They'll love rolling the cabbage leaves. By the way, frozen cabbage peels more easily than unfrozen cabbage.

SERVES 4 TO 6

Preheat the oven to 400°F. Allow the cabbage to thaw slightly, then peel the leaves off. Place 2 to 4 tablespoons of the burger mixture at the edge of each cabbage leaf and roll the leaves into individual logs. Place them in an oblong baking dish.

To make the sauce, combine the butter, tomatoes, carrot, celery, maple syrup, sugar, lemon juice, and oregano. Cover the cabbage rolls with the sauce and bake for about 20 to 30 minutes.

Head of cabbage, frozen overnight

1 recipe Tofu and Cheese Burgers (page 90)

3 tablespoons (1^1/$_2$ ounces) butter, melted

1 24-ounce can plum tomatoes, undrained

1 carrot, thinly chopped

1 celery stalk, thinly chopped

^{1}/$_2$ cup maple syrup

4 tablespoons light brown sugar

3 tablespoons freshly squeezed lemon juice

2 tablespoons dried oregano

Pumpkin and Herbs

3 tablespoons vegetable oil

1 onion, chopped

2 garlic cloves, crushed

2 pounds of pumpkin meat, cut into 1-inch cubes

$^1/_2$ teaspoon dried oregano

$^1/_2$ teaspoon dried thyme

Salt and freshly ground black pepper to taste

$^1/_2$ cup dry sherry

$^1/_4$ cup water

$1^1/_2$ cups cooked black beans

2 cups cooked long grain rice

Most people use pumpkin either to make pumpkin pie or Jack O'Lanterns. We forget, or simply don't realize, that pumpkin is one of the most versatile of vegetables. It can be baked or fried, used in stuffing, or roasted. And it's very nutritious. In this recipe I've combined herbs and spices with the cubed pumpkin to make a wonderful side dish.

SERVES 4

In a sauté pan, in the oil, sauté the onion, garlic, pumpkin, oregano, and thyme for about 10 minutes. Season with the salt and pepper. To the sauté pan, add the sherry, water, and beans and continue cooking until the pumpkin is tender, about 30 minutes. Add the rice and mix well.

Gravy, Salsas, Sauces, Dips, and Side Dishes

Gravy

Gravy. Don't you just love the name? As a kid, I loved biscuits and gravy, gravy on dressing, and, of course, gravy with the meats Mama cooked. Her gravies are all meat-based. It took me years to fig-ure out how to make meatless gravies, but once I got it, I GOT IT. Here are three for you to try: Golden Gravy (below), Pinto Bean Gravy (page 165), and White Gravy (page 166).

Golden Gravy

1 medium onion, finely diced

3 tablespoons olive oil

¹/₂ stick (2 ounces) butter

3 tablespoons all-purpose flour

1 cup vegetable stock (page 20)

Salt and freshly ground black pepper to taste

This gravy is particularly good over any of the dressings or cooked veg-etables found in this book; it adds an extra dimension of flavor to them.

MAKES ABOUT 2 CUPS

In a skillet, sauté the onion in the olive oil until it is brown. Add the butter and lower the heat. As the butter melts, add the flour, stirring constantly to keep it from burning. After the flour browns, add the stock and stir until the gravy thickens. Season with salt and pepper.

Pinto Bean Gravy

This recipe and White Gravy (page 166) are both quite easy. Please don't confuse easy with quick, though. They both take about thirty minutes to make.

MAKES 3 1/2 CUPS

In a pot, bring the beans, water, olive oil, and onion to a boil. Cover and cook for about 30 minutes. Add water if the beans look dry. If the beans begin to boil over, slide the lid slightly to the side to vent. Using a hand-held mixer, purée the beans right in the pot. (If you don't have a hand-held mixer, you can purée the beans in a blender or food processor and return them to the pot before adding the cornstarch.) Mix together the cornstarch and the water and add it to the pot. Stir until the gravy is thickened. Season with salt and pepper.

1 cup pinto beans, soaked overnight and drained

2 cups water

2 tablespoons olive oil

1/2 medium onion, diced

1 teaspoon cornstarch

2 tablespoons water

Salt and freshly ground black pepper to taste

White Gravy

1 cup lima beans, soaked
overnight and drained

1¹/₂ cups water

¹/₄ stick (1 ounce) butter

¹/₂ medium onion, diced

¹/₂ cup heavy cream

1 teaspoon cornstarch

2 tablespoons water

Salt and freshly ground black
pepper to taste

*Using lima beans and cream, you can make a white gravy just as good
as any gravy made with pan drippings.*

MAKES 3 ¹/₂ CUPS

Mix the limas, water, butter, and onion in a saucepan and
bring the mixture to a boil. After 20 minutes, test the beans for
tenderness. If they are not soft, cook an additional 5 to 10
minutes. Add more water if the beans look dry. Remove the
pan from the heat and stir in the cream, using a hand-held
mixer to purée the mixture (or you can purée it in a blender or
food processor). Make a paste by mixing the cornstarch and
water together. Add this to the mixture in the pan over low
heat, stirring until the gravy is as thick as you'd like. Season
with salt and pepper.

Roasted Three Pepper Salsa

〜〜〜

This is a wonderful addition to any grilled item. It's particularly great on veggie burgers (pages 88 to 90).

PARTY SERVING, 4

Mix all the ingredients in a medium bowl. This salsa can be stored in a refrigerator for weeks.

1 red bell pepper, roasted, peeled, cored, seeded, and chopped

1 yellow bell pepper, roasted, peeled, cored, seeded, and chopped

1 green bell pepper, roasted, peeled, cored, seeded, and chopped

1 celery stalk, finely diced

2 tablespoons chopped fresh parsley

2 tablespoons chopped ripe olives

2 tablespoons olive oil

1 tablespoon capers, rinsed and drained

1 teaspoon fresh rosemary

1 garlic clove, minced

Juice of $1/2$ lemon

Salt and freshly ground pepper to taste

Apple Salsa

3 apples, peeled and cored and chopped

¹/₈ cup fresh cilantro, chopped

1 tablespoon chopped fresh mint

1 teaspoon lime rind

1 teaspoon lime juice

1 medium sweet onion, diced

1 tablespoon sugar

¹/₄ cup olive oil

I serve this with both chips and grilled vegetables. It's especially good with Mexican dishes.

PARTY SERVING, 4

Mix all the ingredients together and serve. I prefer a chunky salsa, but you can make it a bit smoother by placing half of the combined mixture in a food processor or blender and chopping it, not puréeing it, for a second or two. Then combine the puréed mixture with the other half of the salsa and mix well.

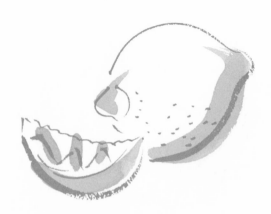

Tomato Salsa

~~~

*Remember . . . salsa is not just for dipping. It's great to smother
sautéed or grilled vegetables in this delicious salsa. And it's wonderful
on sandwiches, or any of the veggie burgers that you will find in this
book. It is especially good over omelettes. I'll let you take it from there.*

PARTY SERVING, 4

Mix all the ingredients together and serve.

3 tomatoes, chopped

4 tablespoons vegetable
  stock (page 20)

2 garlic cloves, chopped

1 jalapeño pepper, chopped

1 tablespoon sugar

2 teaspoons lime juice

$1/2$ cup chopped fresh
  cilantro

Onion Salsa

~~~

*I love this recipe. It can be used in so many ways. Add bread crumbs
and it becomes a stuffing. Purée it with sautéed eggplant and it's a
wonderful dip.*

PARTY SERVING, 4

Heat the oil in a large sauté pan and sauté the leeks, red
onion, green onions, and shallot. Add the garlic, thyme, mayonnaise, and chives and stir to mix. Serve on grilled foods or
with chips.

3 tablespoons olive oil

2 leeks, white part washed
  and finely chopped

1 large red onion, diced

Bunch of green onions,
  all of it chopped

1 shallot, chopped

2 tablespoons minced
  garlic

2 tablespoons fresh thyme

3 tablespoons mayonnaise

2 tablespoons fresh chives

My Marinara

1 medium-to-large onion, diced

3 garlic cloves, minced

1 red bell pepper, diced

4 tablespoons olive oil

1 4-ounce can mushroom pieces, drained

1 24-ounce can whole tomatoes, chopped, the juice reserved

1 pound fresh tomatoes, diced

1 4-ounce can ripe olives, diced

1 6-ounce can tomato paste

2 teaspoons sugar

1 teaspoon salt

$1/2$ teaspoon freshly ground black pepper

$1/2$ teaspoon dried oregano

$1/2$ teaspoon dried basil

2 bay leaves

I use my marinara for everything from pizza to pasta . . . you name it, I put this sauce on it.

MAKES 3 TO 4 CUPS

Sauté the onion, garlic, and red bell pepper in the oil in a large pot for 5 to 7 minutes. Add the mushrooms, canned tomatoes with the juice, and fresh tomatoes, stirring well to combine all of the ingredients. Add the olives, then stir in the tomato paste. Sprinkle the sugar, salt, pepper, oregano, and basil over the mixture and place the bay leaves in the pot. Mix well. Bring the mixture to a boil, lower to simmer, cover, and cook about 2 hours. Remove the bay leaves before serving.

Pumpkin Sauce

Pour this wonderful sauce over grilled vegetables or White Bean Cakes (page 93). The flavor is wonderful and sweet, but not too sweet, and the texture is smooth and creamy, thanks to the whipping cream, of course. If you want to make this as a dessert topping, leave out the garlic and pepper, and substitute melted butter for olive oil. Add 1 1/2 to 2 tablespoons of sugar.

MAKES ABOUT 1 CUP

1 garlic clove, minced

1/4 cup sherry

1 tablespoon olive oil

1/4 cup heavy cream

1/3 cup pumpkin purée

1/4 teaspoon ground nutmeg

Salt and freshly ground black pepper to taste

Sauté the garlic in the sherry and olive oil. Add the remaining ingredients and purée until thick. Heat through.

Cheese Sauce

You can substitute this cheese sauce for the white gravy in Eggplant Enchiladas (page 120). It's also excellent with veggie burgers (pages 88 to 90) and White Bean Cakes (page 93).

MAKES ABOUT 2 CUPS

1/2 stick (2 ounces) butter

1/4 cup all-purpose flour

1 1/2 cups milk

1 cup shredded cheese of your choice

Dash of cayenne pepper

2 tablespoons Worcestershire sauce

Salt and freshly ground black pepper to taste

In a pot, melt the butter, add the flour and stir to make a paste. Add the milk gradually and stir. Add the cheese and other ingredients and stir. Heat until the cheese is melted.

Garlic and Herb Mozzarella

4 ounces chopped fresh
oregano

4 ounces chopped fresh
rosemary

4 ounces chopped fresh
thyme

$^1/_3$ cup olive oil

$^1/_4$ cup canola oil

2 tablespoons ground
ginger

6 garlic cloves, crushed

2 1-pound rounds
mozzarella cheese

A great accompaniment to sliced tomatoes.

SERVES 4

Preheat the oven to 375°F. In a bowl, mix the oregano, rosemary, and thyme with the oils. Add the ginger and garlic and mix well. Pour over the mozzarella rounds in a baking dish and bake for 20 minutes. Serve hot.

Eggplant Dip

Baba ghanoush . . . another name for eggplant dip, and this one is great. Serve it with chips, crackers, or pita bread.

MAKES 2 1/2 TO 3 CUPS

Preheat the oven to 400°F. Bake the eggplant halves for about 45 minutes. Scrape the eggplant pulp from the shells and combine with the yogurt, lemon juice, tahini, garlic, tomato, bell pepper, parsley, and salt and pepper. Purée all the ingredients in a blender or food processor.

2 large eggplants, sliced in half

1/4 cup plain yogurt

Juice of 1 lemon

2 tablespoons tahini

2 cloves garlic, minced

1 ripe tomato, diced

1 green bell pepper or red bell pepper, diced

3 tablespoons minced fresh parsley

Salt and freshly ground black pepper to taste

Hummus

Hummus is fantastic. It can be used as a dip or a sandwich spread. It's great with pita bread. Try it. You'll like it!

MAKES ABOUT 2 1/2 CUPS

Purée all the ingredients together in a food processor or blender.

1 cup cooked garbanzo beans

6 garlic cloves

1/2 cup fresh lemon juice

1 cup tahini paste

Salt and freshly ground black pepper to taste

1/3 cup fresh parsley

Olive Paste or Spread

3 whole green onions, chopped

1 8-ounce can ripe olives, drained well

3 garlic cloves, minced

Juice of 1 lemon

2 ounces plus more ricotta cheese (optional)

Salt and freshly ground black pepper if needed

Whenever I prepare this recipe, I think of my buddy, Jason Seek, in Warrenton, Virginia. I traveled to Warrenton to meet Jason and to speak to his and other schools because of a wonderful letter I received from him. He had seen me on the Home Show, *talking about the difficulties I had in life because I didn't learn to read until the age of twenty-six. Jason, too, was a nonreader. His letter was written by his mom, and it touched me deeply. Jason and his mom took me to a wonderful Italian restaurant and that's where we had this olive paste. Now, thank goodness, Jason is reading; he's in high school, and doing fine. Like me, Jason now loves to read. This spread is great on crackers or toast, and is a wonderful substitute for those of us who don't want to eat meat pâté.*

MAKES ABOUT 2 CUPS

Place all of the ingredients in a food processor or blender and purée. If the mixture is too thin, add 2 ounces or more of ricotta cheese to thicken it. Season with salt and pepper.

Artichoke Paste or Spread

Round artichokes are called globe artichokes, and nearly all the ones grown in this country come from an area just below San Francisco on the California coast. Artichokes are a member of the thistle family, and if you let them stay on the vine long enough, they will blossom. My California garden produces wonderful artichokes. Fresh baby artichoke hearts, which have been steamed about forty minutes, or canned artichoke hearts will work for this recipe. However, it is much simpler to use canned artichoke hearts, and much quicker too. The result is an easy and delicious party dish.

MAKES 2 CUPS

Preheat the oven to 350°F. Combine all the ingredients, pour into a greased baking dish, and bake for 20 to 30 minutes.

1 pound steamed baby artichoke hearts or 2 6-ounce cans artichoke hearts, drained and quartered

1 cup mayonnaise

$1/2$ teaspoon garlic powder

$1/3$ to $1/2$ cup grated Parmesan cheese

2 drops pepper sauce (optional)

Homemade Potato Chips

⟨⟨⟨⟩⟩⟩

1/2 cup vegetable oil
for cooking

1 large potato, peeled
and very thinly sliced
lengthwise

1 teaspoon salt or more
to taste

There's nothing quite like homemade potato chips. If you've never tried them before, you must. They're fabulous. One large potato makes enough chips for two people. Of course, if you're like me, you'll have to use more potatoes because you'll want to share your chips. As you fry these, please remember that just a fraction of the oil is absorbed by the potatoes.

MAKES 2 CUPS

In a heavy pot, heat the oil to about 350°F. Drop about a dozen potato slices at a time into the hot oil, moving them around until they turn golden brown. Scoop them out and place them on a paper towel to drain. Sprinkle them with salt. Repeat with the remaining slices.

Homemade Potato Chips and Blue Cheese Dressing: Recently, I ate at the Buckhead Diner in Atlanta, Georgia, and had something similar to this. Make a batch of Homemade Potato Chips and, while they're hot, drizzle a quarter of a cup or so of one of my blue cheese dressings (pages 82 and 85) over them. I'm telling you . . . you'll love this. If the chips cool, just stick the plate in a warm oven for a minute or two and they'll reheat.

Hash Browns Two Ways

~~~~~~

Growing up in the South, we never had hash browns for breakfast. That's grits country! I became a breakfast–hash brown man only after moving to California. Never one to break with tradition, though, the first thing I do when I get back to Georgia is visit the Waffle House. I order grits . . . and hash browns.

Grated Hash Browns

~~~~~~

Raw potatoes retain more vitamin C than cooked ones.

SERVES 2

Heat the oil in a frying pan. Season the grated potato with salt and pepper. Drop the potato into the frying pan, forming patties with a spatula. Fry on high heat about 4 minutes, turning them once, or until brown on both sides.

2 to 3 tablespoons vegetable oil, for frying

1 large potato, washed, peeled or unpeeled, and grated

Salt and freshly ground black pepper to taste

Country Hash Browns

1 large potato, washed,
peeled or unpeeled,
and diced

2 cups water

salt and freshly ground black
pepper to taste

4 tablespoons vegetable
oil, for frying

These are wonderful by themselves, but you can jazz them up by adding diced pepper and onion as they cook.

SERVES 2

Parboil the potato in the water for 10 to 15 minutes. Drain and cool it. Sprinkle the potato with salt and pepper. Heat the oil in a frying pan and fry the potato until it is golden brown.

Scalloped Potatoes with Gruyère

Talk about a comfort food. Scalloped potatoes definitely fall in this category. Don't worry about your diet with this dish.

SERVES 4 TO 6

Preheat the oven to 350°F and grease a baking dish. On the bottom of the baking dish, make a layer of potato slices, then cover it with a layer of the onion. Sprinkle half of the cheese over the onion, followed by half of the flour. Dot the flour with half of the butter. Continue layering until the potato slices, onion, cheese, flour, and butter are used up. Mix the cream and milk together and pour over the top. Season with a bit of salt and pepper. Bake for 1½ to 2 hours until the liquid has thickened.

8 medium potatoes, peeled or unpeeled, thinly sliced

1 large onion, chopped

$^1/_2$ to $^3/_4$ cup grated Gruyère cheese

$^1/_3$ cup all-purpose flour

$^1/_2$ stick (2 ounces) butter

$^1/_2$ cup heavy cream

2 cups milk

Salt and freshly ground black pepper to taste

Sautéed Carrots

2 tablespoons olive oil

1 tablespoon butter

2 pounds carrots, peeled and sliced diagonally

2 garlic cloves, minced

2 teaspoons dried oregano

2 teaspoons fresh parsley

¹/₃ cup marsala

¹/₄ cup grated Parmesan cheese, for garnish

A six-inch carrot contains five thousand units of vitamin A. This dish is a great way to get your kids to take their vitamins.

SERVES 3 TO 4

In a saucepan, heat the oil and butter and add the carrots, garlic, oregano, and parsley. Cook 5 to 8 minutes. Add the marsala and cook until the liquid reduces, about 5 minutes. Sprinkle the Parmesan cheese over the top and serve.

Mama's Cabbage

Normally, I think of this as a side dish, not a soup, but for the last year or so I've been eating it as a soup. When I'm in Georgia, I'll call Mama and say, "How about some corn bread and cabbage?" You might think this is like corned beef and cabbage. It isn't at all. It's exactly what it sounds like: a big pan of corn bread and a pot of cabbage. The baked corn bread is crumbled up into the cabbage, juice and all. For those of you who don't know, we Southerners call the juices in a pot of cooked vegetables "pot likker," and yes, that's how we spell it, too. It must be because the juices are so good you feel drunk with delight but don't get a hangover. As with so many of Mama's basic foods, you can use cooked cabbage with the pot likker as a vegetable stock. Just add any combination of chopped onion, tomatoes, or potatoes. Give it a try and let me know the results. (You can also make this recipe using red cabbage.)

SERVES 3 OR 1 OF ME

$^1/_2$ to 1 cup water

1 small or medium green cabbage, cut up

4 tablespoons corn oil

Salt and freshly ground black pepper to taste

In a medium saucepan, bring the water to a boil, using ½ cup for a small cabbage and 1 cup for a medium cabbage. Add the cabbage and the oil. Cover and cook about 15 minutes. The cabbage should be soft. Season with salt and pepper. Serve with plenty of hot corn bread.

Cabbage and Apples

1 stick (4 ounces) butter

1 medium onion, chopped

2 apples, peeled, cored, and sliced

2 tablespoons light brown sugar

1/2 tablespoon ground cloves

1/2 tablespoon ground cinnamon

Juice of 1 lemon

Salt and freshly ground black pepper to taste

Head of red cabbage, cored and shredded

1/2 cup red wine

Please don't let this combination scare you. This is a wonderful dish, take my word for it. No, don't take my word for it, try it yourself. The taste is wonderful.

SERVES 4

In a large sauté pan, melt the butter and sauté the onion until it is translucent. Add the apples, brown sugar, cloves, cinnamon, lemon juice, and salt and pepper. Toss well to combine. Add the cabbage and red wine. Cook 10 to 15 minutes until the cabbage is tender.

Great Beans

The key to making great vegetarian beans is what I call "making the flavor." The traditional soul food–style of cooking beans is with ham hocks, other cuts of pork, or with just plain pork fat. Not only does the fat flavor the meat, it also creates the heartburn many of us get later on. I'm going to share several ways of making the flavor without the animal fat. You will love the results and so will your digestive system.

Black-eyed Peas

1 pound dried black-eyed
  peas, soaked overnight

1/2 stick (2 ounces) butter or
  margarine

1 large onion, cut into big
  cubes

1 large shallot, quartered

3 to 4 cups water

1/4 green bell pepper, cored,
  seeded, and chopped

1 teaspoon salt

1/2 teaspoon freshly ground
  black pepper

This is a traditional dish Mama would cook with pork and serve on Sunday after church. It is a dish I have always loved. In the eighties when I stopped eating red meat, Mama started using chicken to flavor the black-eyed peas, and the family seems to like this version even better. My recipe, though, is totally meatless and truly outstanding. If you don't like these peas, something must be wrong with your taste buds!

SERVES 4

Drain the peas, discarding the water, and set them aside.

Making the Flavor: In a large skillet over medium heat, put the butter, onion, and shallot. When the butter is melted, increase the heat and add the peas. Mix with a wooden spoon, cover, and cook about 8 minutes.

Pour the contents of the skillet into a large pot, adding enough water to cover the peas. Bring to a boil and add the green bell pepper, salt, and black pepper. Lower the heat to medium and cook 50 to 60 minutes, or until the peas are tender.

White Beans (Limas)

These beans are to live for! They are great with just corn bread, and with corn bread, onions, and tomatoes. They're wonderful with broccoli and great as a side dish or as the main part of the meal.

SERVES 4

Drain the beans, discarding the water, and set them aside in a large pot.

Making the Flavor: In a saucepan over medium-to-high heat, put the oil, tomatoes, garlic, and basil. Stir and cover. Cook 6 to 8 minutes.

Add the tomato mixture to the beans, cover, and place over medium heat. Take care not to let the beans dry out, adding ¼ cup of the water at a time as necessary. Cook for 30 minutes. Then add the remaining water and the salt and pepper. Lower the heat and simmer, covered, for another 60 minutes, or until the beans are tender. If more cooking time is needed, just add another ¼ cup of water.

1 pound limas, soaked overnight

6 tablespoons olive oil

2 large tomatoes, peeled and diced

5 garlic cloves, minced or finely chopped

6 ounces fresh basil (or 3 ounces dried basil)

½ cup water

1 teaspoon salt

½ teaspoon freshly ground black pepper

Pinto Beans

1 pound pinto beans, soaked overnight

3 cups vegetable stock (page 20)

3 to 4 tablespoons butter

3 to 4 cups water

1 whole shallot

1 teaspoon salt

1/2 teaspoon freshly ground black pepper

This recipe uses butter; for a fat-free version, just leave the butter out. I have to tell you, though, those few grams of fat add lots of flavor.

SERVES 4

Drain the beans, discarding the water, and place them in a large pot.

Making the Flavor: Pour the stock over the beans and bring to a boil. Add half the butter and boil about 5 to 7 minutes, covered. Add the water and shallot and return to a boil. Lower the heat and simmer for 60 minutes. Add the remaining butter and salt and pepper. Cook another hour until the beans are tender.

Red Beans and Rice

I first tried red beans and rice when I went off to college at Southern University in Baton Rouge, Louisiana. It seemed to me this dish was a daily staple in Louisiana. Certainly that was true at the training table where I sat at mealtimes. I fell in love with those beans which, as you might have guessed, were made with pounds of pork and pork fat. Here's my meatless version of that Louisiana classic.

SERVES 3 TO 5

Drain the beans, discarding the water, and set them aside in a pot.

Making the Flavor: Place the onion, celery, garlic, and bay leaves in a medium mixing bowl. Drizzle the olive oil over them and let the mixture sit at room temperature for at least 30 minutes.

Then pour the oil and vegetables over the beans and let sit at room temperature for 10 to 15 minutes. Add enough of the water to cover the beans and bring to a boil. Lower the heat to simmer, add the salt and pepper, cover, and cook until the beans are tender, about 3 to 4 hours. Remove the bay leaves and serve the hot beans over the rice.

1 pound dried red beans, soaked overnight

1 large yellow onion, diced

$1^1/_2$ celery stalks, diced

4 garlic cloves, finely chopped or minced

2 bay leaves

$^3/_4$ cup olive oil

3 to 4 cups water

1 teaspoon salt

$^1/_2$ teaspoon freshly ground black pepper

2 to 3 cups cooked rice

Good Green Beans

2 to 3 cups water, enough to just cover the beans

2 pounds green beans, cut into 1-inch pieces

1 medium onion, whole or diced

2 tablespoons oil

Salt and freshly ground black pepper to taste

Most of us think of green beans as a side dish, and they certainly are that. These are a classic Southern side dish. But some of the best soups I've ever eaten have used this recipe as a soup stock base.

SERVES 6 TO 8 EASILY

Bring the water to a boil. Add the beans, onion (whole if you want the onion flavor without the onion pieces—you remove it at the end; or diced if you want to serve onion pieces with the green beans), and oil. Cover and cook over medium heat about 40 minutes. Season with salt and pepper and cook another 20 minutes, covered for more pot likker, uncovered for less.

White Beans and Vegetables

This is an easy recipe using canned beans, artichoke hearts, and tomatoes. You can, of course, use fresh vegetables and rehydrated beans, but you will need to add about another hour of cooking time. This is delicious either way.

SERVES 6 TO 8 EASILY

In a large saucepan, heat 2 tablespoons of the olive oil. Add the garlic and onion and sauté about 4 minutes. Add the remaining 2 teaspoons of oil and the remaining ingredients except the orzo. Cook 10 to 15 minutes or until the mixture is thoroughly hot and the vegetables are tender. Add the orzo and mix well.

1/4 cup olive oil

2 to 3 garlic cloves, minced

2 cups chopped onion

2 cups diced carrots

1 red bell pepper, diced

1 medium crookneck squash, diced

1 tablespoon chopped fresh dill

1 tablespoon chopped fresh mint

1 tablespoon butter

1 8-ounce can artichoke hearts, drained and chopped

3 cups white kidney beans, cooked (also called cannellini beans)

1 8-ounce can Italian stewed tomatoes

3/4 pound orzo pasta, cooked

My Version of Mama's Corn Bread Dressing

~~~~~~

4 cups crumbled Mama's
  Corn Bread (page 3)

2 cups toasted bread, cut into
  1-inch cubes

10 saltine crackers, crumbled

2 cups vegetable stock
  (page 20)

3 celery stalks, diced

1 medium onion, diced

2 large eggs

1/2 stick (2 ounces) butter

1 teaspoon dried sage

Salt and freshly ground black
  pepper to taste

As a kid, I don't ever remember my mama making stuffing for the bird at Thanksgiving. Instead, she made what Southerners call "dressing," and it was baked in a large roasting pan. I have no idea where the name comes from, but I do love the dish. This side dish of my meat-eating childhood has become a main dish of my meatless adulthood. Top it with gravy (page 164).

SERVES 6 TO 8 EASILY

Preheat the oven to 350°F and lightly grease an 8-inch baking dish. Combine the corn bread, toasted bread, and crackers in a large mixing bowl. Pour the stock into a saucepan and add the celery and onion. Bring to a boil and cook for 10 to 15 minutes. Remove the stock mixture from the stove and allow it to cool for about 10 minutes before proceeding. When it has cooled, add the stock mixture to the bread crumb mixture along with the eggs, butter, sage, and salt and pepper. Mix well. Pour into the baking dish and bake 1½ hours or longer until the dressing is set and nicely browned.

Curtis's Rice Dressing

Rice dressing is very popular with Creole and Cajun cooks in
Louisiana. It's also very popular with me, though my version isn't hot
and spicy like the bayou variety. This can be a side dish or a main part
of a meal. It's great with a little vegetarian gravy over it too.

SERVES 4 TO 6

Preheat the oven to 350°F. In a large mixing bowl, combine all the ingredients and mix well. Pour the mixture into a greased baking dish or Dutch oven with a lid. Bake 1½ hours, covered, and an additional 10 to 15 minutes, uncovered.

1 cup raw rice

2 cups soup (I use vegetable)

$^1/_2$ cup water

5 whole green onions, chopped

$^1/_2$ medium red onion, diced

$^1/_2$ yellow bell pepper, diced

10 Ritz crackers, crumbled

Salt and freshly ground black pepper to taste

Potato Dressing

2 cups crumbled Mama's
  Corn Bread (page 3)

2 cups toasted bread,
  crumbled

10 saltine crackers, crumbled

2 cups vegetable stock
  (page 20)

1 cup water

2 potatoes, peeled and cubed

3 celery stalks, diced

1 medium onion, diced

2 large eggs

$^1/_2$ stick (2 ounces) butter

1 teaspoon dried sage

1 teaspoon dried rosemary

$^1/_2$ teaspoon dried thyme

Salt and freshly ground black
  pepper to taste

Many of my recipes are created out of necessity. I was making my version of corn bread dressing one evening and found I didn't have enough corn bread. Potatoes make a good stretcher, and the results were so tasty, this Potato Dressing has become one of my favorite dishes. Serve it with gravy (page 164), and you'll love it too.

SERVES 4 TO 6 EASILY

Preheat the oven to 375°F. Grease an oblong baking dish and set it aside. Combine the corn bread, toasted bread, and crackers in a large mixing bowl. In a saucepan, bring to a boil the stock, water, and potatoes. Cook about 8 minutes. Reserving the stock, drain off the potatoes and set them aside. Allow the stock to cool for 10 minutes. Add the stock, celery, onion, eggs, butter, sage, rosemary, and thyme to the bread mixture and mix well. Pour the potatoes into the baking dish and sprinkle them with the salt and pepper. Cover the potatoes with the dressing mixture. Allow about 5 minutes for the dressing to fall in between the potatoes. Bake 1½ to 2 hours and serve topped with gravy.

Desserts

Apple Bundt Cake

8 medium apples, peeled, cored, and diced

1¹/₂ to 2 cups sugar

¹/₂ cup vegetable oil

2 teaspoons vanilla extract

2 large eggs, slightly beaten

2 cups all-purpose flour

2 teaspoons baking soda

1 teaspoon ground nutmeg

1 teaspoon ground cinnamon

Dash of salt

¹/₂ cup pecan pieces

There have been over seven thousand varieties of apples cultivated since Adam and Eve's stay in the Garden of Eden. You need only one for this recipe. However, I feel a combination of three works best, such as Granny Smith, red Delicious, and Winesap, or any combination of locally grown apples. This is a cake that stores very well. You can make it today, and it will still be good five days later if you keep it wrapped in your cake safe. Excellent in the kids' lunches.

SERVES 6 TO 8

Preheat the oven to 350°F. Grease and flour a Bundt pan. In a large mixing bowl, place the apples, sugar, vegetable oil, and vanilla. Stir to mix and let stand 5 to 10 minutes. Add the beaten eggs and mix. In another bowl, sift together the flour, baking soda, nutmeg, cinnamon, and salt. Combine the dry ingredients with the apple mixture, adding the pecans and mixing well. Bake for 50 to 60 minutes, or until a toothpick inserted in the cake comes out clean. This cake is great served with strawberries.

Carrot Cake

You've heard me say on many occasions that my mama is the best cook I know. But Mama would be the first to tell you she's not the best cake baker . . . she's pretty good, but not the best. That would be Mrs. Gwinell Read. She passed away a few years ago, but the memory of her cakes will live forever with a lot of folks around Conyers.

SERVES 6 TO 8

Preheat the oven to 375°F. Grease and flour 2 baking pans. In a large bowl, combine the sugar, oil, and carrot juice. Add the eggs and mix well. In another bowl, sift together the flour, baking powder, baking soda, cinnamon, and salt. Add the dry ingredients to the wet ingredients, stirring in the carrots. Pour into the prepared pans and bake for about 45 minutes, or until an inserted straw or toothpick withdraws cleanly. Allow the cake to cool before icing.

In a bowl, beat together the butter and cream cheese until fluffy. Add the vanilla and sugar and beat until the ingredients combine and the icing is smooth. Don't overbeat. Spread over the cake and sprinkle with finely grated orange rind. This icing is also wonderful on the Apple Bundt Cake (page 194).

FOR THE CAKE

2 cups sugar

1 cup vegetable oil

$^1/_2$ cup carrot juice

4 large eggs, beaten

2 cups all-purpose flour

3 teaspoons baking powder

2 teaspoons baking soda

2 teaspoons ground cinnamon

$^1/_4$ teaspoon salt

1 pound carrots, peeled and grated

FOR THE ICING:

$^3/_4$ stick butter, softened

10 ounces cream cheese

2 teaspoons vanilla extract

$2^1/_2$ cups powdered sugar

4 tablespoons grated orange rind, for garnish

Homemade Pie Crust

1¹/₂ cups all-purpose flour

Dash of salt

¹/₂ cup vegetable
  shortening

¹/₂ cup ice-cold water

Mama always keeps a couple of frozen pie crusts on hand, but only for emergency use. Most of the time she whips up her own, using flour, shortening, and ice water.

MAKES ONE 9-INCH PIE CRUST

Place the flour and salt in a mixing bowl. Add the shortening and cut it in with a pastry blender, or use your hands, as I do. Add the water, a tablespoonful at a time, kneading until the dough is smooth. Roll out the dough to fit a 9-inch pie pan.

Baked Banana Pie

Bananas are high on my list of favorite fruits . . . which is why I've included several recipes in this dessert chapter. For this banana pie, use fresh pineapple juice. The flavor is outstanding and so refreshing with the bananas. You might want to serve this pie with a little bit of ice cream (chocolate).

MAKES ONE 9-INCH PIE

Preheat the oven to 400°F. Soak the sliced bananas in the pineapple juice for 20 to 30 minutes. Drain, reserve the juice, then place the bananas in a pastry-lined pie plate. Add the sugar and cinnamon which have been mixed together. Add 2 teaspoons of pineapple juice. Dot with the butter and cover with a top crust. Bake for 30 to 45 minutes, or until crust is brown.

4 cups ripe but firm sliced bananas

$1/2$ cup pineapple juice

2 recipes Homemade Pie Crust (page 196)

$3/4$ cup sugar

1 teaspoon ground cinnamon

3 tablespoons ($1^1/_2$ ounces) butter or margarine

Pineapple and Orange Pie or Maui Pie

2 cups chopped fresh pineapple, with the juice retained

2 packages unflavored gelatin

2 cups orange sections, cut into pieces

1 can sweetened condensed milk

2 large egg whites

¹/₄ teaspoon cream of tartar

³/₄ cup chopped toasted macadamia nuts

1 baked recipe Homemade Pie Crust (page 196)

This is my version of a pie I had in a restaurant in upcountry Maui. The combination of local fresh oranges and sun-ripened Maui pineapples is wonderful when they're sliced and eaten from a bowl, so just imagine it as a pie. I hope you find it as delightful as I do.

MAKES ONE 9-INCH PIE

From chopping the pineapple, you should have at least ¹/₄ cup juice. If not, add orange juice or water to make that amount. Put the pineapple juice and gelatin in a small saucepan and cook until the gelatin dissolves, stirring constantly until it is dissolved. In a mixing bowl, put the pineapple, orange pieces, and milk. Mix well. Stir in the gelatin. By hand or with an electric mixer, beat together the egg whites and cream of tartar until stiff peaks form. Fold into the pineapple mixture. Spread half the macadamia nuts evenly over the bottom of the pie crust. Add the pie filling and sprinkle the remaining macadamia nuts over the top of it. Chill until the pie is firm. Slice and serve.

Pecan Pie

I believe there are as many variations of pecan pie as there are Mamas to make them, and I'm equally sure every mama's pecan pie tastes great. Here's one that's pretty simple and very good.

MAKES ONE 9-INCH PIE

Preheat the oven to 375°F. In a large bowl, beat the eggs with the sugar, corn syrup, and butter. Add the salt and stir to mix. Line the bottom of the pie shell with the pecan halves and pour the egg mixture over the pecans. Bake for 30 to 40 minutes until the pecans rise to the top and the pie is firm.

4 large eggs

1 cup sugar

³/₄ cup corn syrup

2 tablespoons butter, melted

Dash of salt

1 cup pecan halves

1 unbaked recipe Homemade Pie Crust (page 196)

Pineapple Pecan Pie

3 large eggs

1 cup corn syrup

$^1/_2$ cup light brown sugar

$^1/_2$ stick (2 ounces) butter, melted

$^1/_2$ fresh pineapple, crushed (drain off the juice)

1 cup pecans

1 unbaked recipe Homemade Pie Crust (page 196)

I love to combine pecan and dried pineapple chunks in trail mixes, and I feel the two flavors work even better in pies. Oh, by the way, the pineapple is the international symbol of welcome, and the pecan is a nut native to the southern part of our country, which is also known for its hospitality. I feel the pie works much better with fresh pineapple, but if it is not available, feel free to substitute canned.

MAKES ONE 9-INCH PIE

Preheat the oven to 375°F. Beat the eggs until light and fluffy. Add the corn syrup, sugar, and butter. Mix until the sugar dissolves. Stir in the pineapple and pecans. Pour into the pie shell. Bake 45 to 50 minutes. Cool and serve.

Apple Pie

What's more American than apple pie? Probably lots of things, these days. But apple pie will always be one of my favorite comfort foods. It's easy to make, just take your time with the crust.

MAKES ONE 9-INCH PIE

Preheat the oven to 375°F. Place the apples, sugar, cinnamon, and nutmeg in a mixing bowl. Mix well and let the mixture sit at room temperature while you prepare the pie crust. Fit one pie crust in the bottom of a pie pan. Pinch the edges and poke holes in the crust with a fork to keep it from buckling during baking. Pour the apple mixture into the crust. Dot all but about 1 teaspoon of butter on top of the apples. Place the second pie crust on top of the pie. Pinch the edges together. Slit the top for ventilation. Spread the remaining teaspoon of butter on the top. Bake for about 45 to 55 minutes.

2 pounds apples, peeled, cored, and sliced

1 cup sugar

$1/2$ teaspoon ground cinnamon

$1/2$ teaspoon ground nutmeg

2 unbaked recipes Homemade Pie Crust (page 196)

$3/4$ stick (3 ounces) butter, cut into pieces

Strawberry Pie

~~~~~

1 pound strawberries, whole or halved

4 tablespoons cornstarch

1 cup sugar

3 tablespoons water

Dash of salt

$^1/_2$ tablespoon butter

1 baked recipe Homemade Pie Crust (page 196)

This pie is one of those cool, refreshing kinds of desserts. It makes me think of California because of the wonderful berries grown from Watsonville, south of San Francisco, to Oxnard, north of Los Angeles. And I think also of Georgia and remember Mama's strawberry pies.

MAKES ONE 9-INCH PIE

In a saucepan, place about a third of the strawberries along with the cornstarch, sugar, water, salt, and butter. Cook over medium heat about 10 minutes, stirring constantly to avoid burning. When the mixture looks like jam, it's ready. Place the remaining strawberries in the pie crust and cover with the cooled cooked strawberries. Chill and serve plain or topped with whipped cream.

Pumpkin Pie

If you can't find fresh pumpkin, butternut or Hubbard squash is a great substitute. Your guests will never know. In this recipe, I've used some pumpkin pie spice. It is a combination of equal amounts of ground cinnamon and nutmeg, and one third the amount of cloves, with a dash of allspice.

MAKES ONE 9-INCH PIE

Preheat the oven to 375°F. While the pumpkin is still hot, mash it with the sugar and butter. Add the milk and stir to combine. Mix in the eggs and pie spice. Pour into the pie crust and bake about 1 hour.

2^1/$_4$ cups cooked pumpkin

1 cup sugar

^{3}/$_4$ stick (3 ounces) butter

^{1}/$_2$ cup milk

3 large eggs, beaten

2 teaspoons pumpkin pie spice

1 recipe Homemade Pie Crust (page 196)

Sweet Potato Pie

2 medium sweet potatoes,
 peeled and diced

1¹/₂ to 2 cups water

1 stick (4 ounces) butter

³/₄ to 1 cup sugar

2 large eggs, beaten

¹/₄ cup buttermilk

¹/₂ teaspoon vanilla extract

1 unbaked recipe Homemade
 Pie Crust (page 196)

I do believe every African-American mother knows how to make sweet potato pie, and if she has a son, he does too. Here is one I learned from mine.

MAKES ONE 9-INCH PIE

Preheat the oven to 325°F. Place the potatoes in a saucepan covered with the water. Bring to a boil and cook 15 to 20 minutes, or until the potatoes are tender and soft. Drain and discard the water. While the potatoes are still hot, mash them with the butter and sugar. Let this mixture cool slightly, then add the beaten eggs along with the buttermilk and vanilla and combine well. Pour into the pie crust and bake for about 1 hour.

Mud Pie

Mud pie is truly a Southern favorite. It varies from state to state, county to county. But I have a confession. Mama never prepared it while I was growing up. And the first time I had mud pie was in California. I will tell you, I made up for all those bites I missed in my childhood. Here's my rendition of mud pie.

MAKES ONE 9-INCH PIE

In a freezer-proof dish, crumble the cookies and pour the butter over them. Add a layer of coffee ice cream and top with the fudge, then the almonds. Freeze solid before serving.

12 to 16 oreo cookies (8 to 10 ounces)

3 tablespoons (1 1/2 ounces) butter, melted

1/2 gallon coffee ice cream

6 ounces fudge (more or less)

4 ounces sliced toasted almonds

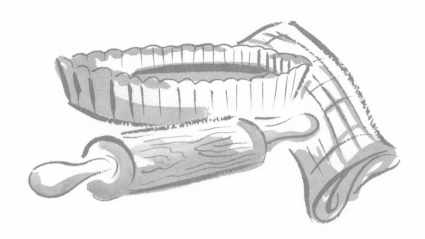

Cherry Pastry

2 16-ounce cans pitted cherries, chopped, with ½ cup syrup reserved

¼ cup all-purpose flour

¼ cup sugar

2 tablespoons cornmeal

½ teaspoon baking powder

½ teaspoon ground cinnamon or ground cloves

2 large eggs

Confectioners' sugar, for garnish

I love fresh cherries, but I've got to tell you, cooking with them is a major pain, so here's one of those rare times I would say use canned fruit. Not because it tastes better . . . it just saves you hours and lots of stains. You know what, just for the thrill of it when making this dessert, buy about a pound of fresh Bing or Royal Ann cherries for the kids to enjoy while watching you work . . . and for you to enjoy too.

SERVES 4 TO 6 EASILY

Preheat the oven to 375°F. Lightly grease a 9-inch deep-dish pie plate.

Drain the cherries and reserve ½ cup of the syrup. Put the flour, sugar, cornmeal, baking powder, and cinnamon into a bowl. Stir to mix well. In separate bowl, lightly beat the eggs. Stir them and then the reserved syrup into flour mixture. Stir in chopped cherries. Pour the batter into the prepared pan and bake 40 to 45 minutes, until a pick inserted in center comes out clean. Sprinkle with confectioners' sugar.

Blackberry Cobbler

During the summers of my preteen years, my brother Jeffrey and I would spend many days picking berries in the backyard to take in to Mama for to make her blackberry cobbler. I do believe we ate more berries than we took into the house, but Mama always had enough to prepare a cobbler. If you want to make another kind of fruit cobbler, just substitute an equal amount of some other fruit for the blackberries, and season appropriately to the fruit. For instance, if you're using apples or pears, you might try a bit of nutmeg.

SERVES 6 TO 8 EASILY

1 to 1$^1/_2$ pounds blackberries

1 to 1$^1/_2$ cups sugar

1$^1/_2$ tablespoons all-purpose flour

2 tablespoons vanilla extract

$^3/_4$ cup water

$^3/_4$ stick butter, cut into pieces

1 unbaked recipe Homemade Pie Crust (page 196)

Preheat the oven to 350°F. Place the blackberries in a baking dish. In a bowl, combine the sugar and flour and sprinkle the mixture over the blackberries. In another bowl, mix the vanilla and water and drizzle over all, dotting the top with the butter pieces. Place the crust on top of the blackberries. It does not have to come to the edges of the baking dish . . . in fact, it's better if it doesn't. Bake for 45 to 55 minutes.

Homemade Cookie Crust

1 cup chopped cookie crumbs
(your favorite kind)

1/4 cup sugar

3/4 stick (3 ounces) butter,
melted

This can be used as a crust for any pie, especially fruit pies.

MAKES ONE 9-INCH CRUST

Mix together all the ingredients. Press mixture into a
9-inch pie pan. Chill until ready to use.

Benne Wafers

3/4 cup (6 ounces) butter,
softened

1 cup light brown sugar

1 large egg

1 teaspoon vanilla extract

1/2 cup benne (sesame) seeds

1 1/2 cups sifted all-purpose
flour

1/2 teaspoon baking powder

*This is a dessert that is very famous and popular in South Carolina.
Benne was the name given to the sesame seed by Africans forced into
slavery. It has a delightful, nutty flavor and is crisp to the bite. When I
think of soul food, the benne wafer and cooked okra are two of the
things that come to mind.*

MAKES ABOUT TWO DOZEN WAFERS

Preheat the oven to 375°F. In a bowl, mix the butter,
sugar, egg, and vanilla. Stir in the dry ingredients. Drop the
dough by the teaspoonful onto a cookie sheet. Bake 10 minutes.

Banana Papaya Muffins

This recipe combines all the best of Hawaii for me. My friends there have papaya, banana, mango, and macadamia nut trees growing in their backyard, and every time I am there, I come up with all kinds of combinations for Mother Nature's bountiful harvest. The banana and papaya make a natural marriage, and added macadamia nuts make them just that much more rich and satisfying.

MAKES 8 TO 12

Preheat the oven to 325°F. Cream the sugar with the butter until it is a light yellow color. Add the eggs and beat until fluffy. Add the banana, papaya, macadamia nuts, and raisins and mix. Sift the flour with the baking powder, baking soda, salt, cinnamon, allspice, and ginger. Add to the banana papaya mixture. Fill lined muffin pans three quarters full and bake for 25 minutes.

1 cup sugar

$^1/_2$ cup (4 ounces) butter

2 large eggs

$^1/_2$ cup mashed banana

$^1/_2$ cup mashed papaya

$^1/_4$ cup chopped macadamia nuts

$^1/_2$ cup raisins

$1^1/_2$ cups all-purpose flour

$^1/_4$ teaspoon baking powder

1 teaspoon baking soda

$^1/_2$ teaspoon salt

$^1/_2$ teaspoon ground cinnamon

$^1/_2$ teaspoon ground allspice

$^1/_2$ teaspoon ground ginger

Banana Bread

2 cups sugar

$^1/_2$ cup (4 ounces) butter

$^1/_2$ cup vegetable
  shortening

6 ripe bananas, mashed

4 large eggs, beaten

$2^1/_2$ cups all-purpose flour

2 teaspoons baking soda

1 teaspoon salt

$^1/_2$ cup mixed nuts, chopped

Just in the last few years, the banana has become this country's number one fruit, unseating the longtime king, the apple. Bananas are at their highest sugar level when they become brown-spotted. To slow the ripening process, place bananas in the refrigerator. The skin will turn brown, but the flesh stays nice and white. If you don't eat the bananas within two or three days, slice or mash them, place them in a plastic bag, and freeze them. You will then have bananas on hand for baking at any time.

SERVES 6 TO 8

Preheat the oven to 350°F. Grease and flour a loaf pan. In a large mixing bowl, place the sugar, butter, and shortening and beat until the mixture is creamy. Add the bananas and eggs and mix well. In another bowl, sift together the flour, baking soda, and salt and add to the banana mixture along with the nuts. Stir to combine well. Pour into the prepared pan and bake about 1 hour.

Mango Macadamia Nut Bread

I love visiting my friends in Maui: Tim and Helen in Makawo; Dorothy, Roxanna, and Pat in Lahina. And I truly enjoy being able to go out in their yards and pick from their trees what we mainlanders think of as exotic fruit: mango, papaya, avocado, and macadamia nuts. I created this bread with my Maui family in mind.

SERVES 6 TO 8

Preheat the oven to 350°F. Grease and flour a loaf pan. In a bowl, cream the butter and sugar together. Add the eggs and mix well. Add the mango, orange juice, coconut, and macadamia nuts and combine. In another bowl, sift together the flour, baking soda, salt, and cinnamon. Add the dry ingredients to the mango mixture. Stir until the batter combines. Pour into the loaf pan and bake about 1 hour.

¹/₂ cup (4 ounces) butter

1 cup sugar

3 large eggs

1¹/₂ cups diced mango

2 teaspoons orange juice

¹/₂ cup grated coconut

¹/₂ cup chopped macadamia nuts

2 cups all-purpose flour

1 teaspoon baking soda

1 teaspoon salt

1 teaspoon ground cinnamon

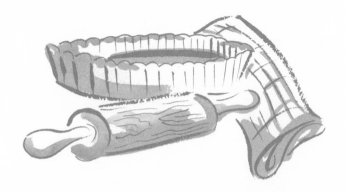

Hot Fudge Pudding

FOR THE BATTER

1 cup flour

3/4 cup sugar

2 tablespoons cocoa

3 teaspoons baking powder

1/4 teaspoon salt

1/2 cup milk

1 cup chopped nuts

1 teaspoon vanilla extract

1/4 stick (1 ounce) butter, melted.

FOR THE TOPPING

1 cup light brown sugar

1 1/3 cups hot water

4 tablespoons cocoa

If you like chocolate like I like chocolate, oh, oh, oh, what a dessert! Now the truth about this recipe, folks, is that one night I was having a dessert fit, and I rambled through my cupboards, and all I had was flour, sugar, and cocoa, so I built this chocolate pudding and it worked. I have enhanced it since by adding nuts and milk. Let me know what you think of it after you try it.

SERVES 6 TO 8

Preheat the oven to 350°F. In a bowl, sift the flour, sugar, cocoa, baking powder, and salt together. Add the milk, nuts, vanilla, and butter and mix until smooth. Pour into a 9 × 13-inch baking pan. Mix the brown sugar, water, and cocoa well and pour over the batter. Bake for about 45 minutes.

Banana Pudding

When I was a kid and Mama made banana pudding, I would eat so much I'd get sick. That never stopped me from going back for more. She made a huge pudding. The pudding I make these days is smaller.

SERVES 6 EASILY

In a bowl, place a layer of sliced bananas followed by a layer of vanilla wafers. Repeat the layers until all the bananas and wafers are used up, ending with a layer of wafers. In a saucepan, place the egg, sugar, and flour and stir to combine. Add the milk and vanilla. Bring to a boil, stirring constantly until the mixture thickens. Pour the pudding mixture over the bananas and wafers, chill, and serve.

1¹/₂ pounds bananas, peeled and sliced

6 to 8 ounces vanilla wafers

1 large egg, slightly beaten

¹/₂ cup sugar

2 teaspoons all-purpose flour

1 cup milk

¹/₂ teaspoon vanilla extract

Bermuda Banana Pudding

~~~~~

1 tablespoon butter

3¹/₂ teaspoons light brown sugar

4 cups mashed bananas

2 tablespoons all-purpose flour

¹/₄ cup milk

There are very few cooked banana dishes I don't enjoy. This is one I love, especially with the brown sugar and butter, which add a caramel flavor to it. I had it for the first time while on a romantic getaway in Bermuda. There it was made with the little Bermuda finger bananas. These can be difficult to find outside Bermuda, so use either yellow bananas or, if available, red bananas.

SERVES 4 TO 6

Preheat the oven to 375°F. Cream the butter and sugar. Add the bananas and mix well. Add the flour and milk and mix. Pour into a greased 9-inch pie pan. Bake for about 45 minutes.

Caramel Sauce

~~~~

I thought I should include a recipe for an easy caramel sauce since it's so good on so many things. It's great over mixed fruit and ice cream, to dip apples in, or smeared on top of Banana Papaya Muffins (page 209). It's also good on top of custards, omelets (for a sweet), French toast, and even pancakes.

MAKES 1 1/3 CUPS

In a saucepan, melt the butter. Add the sugar, then the cream and nuts. Stir until the sugar is melted.

$1/3$ cup butter

$1/3$ cup light brown sugar

$1/3$ cup cream

$1/3$ cup nuts

Carambola

4 tablespoons ground
cinnamon

2 bananas, sliced

1 starfruit, sliced

1 tablespoon sugar

1 stick (4 ounces) butter or
margarine

4 slices of raisin nut bread

Carambola (starfruit) can be eaten by itself but it's used primarily as a garnish because it's so pretty. It adds a delightful, refreshing sweet-tart flavor to many dishes and desserts. If you're not a fan of raisin bread, feel free to substitute pound cake, shortcakes, or lady fingers. Carambola is excellent over ice cream too.

SERVES 4

In a pan, sauté the cinnamon, bananas, starfruit, and sugar in the butter until warm, about 1½ minutes. Place 1 slice of bread on each plate and cover it with the fruit mixture. Top with chocolate syrup and whipped cream.

Epilogue

To my friends, old and new . . . all of you:

A year or so ago, when I did an interview with *TV Guide*, I was asked where my love of cooking came from. I said, "Mama, of course." She taught me not only to love cooking, but also the passing and sharing of love through cooking. My television work and my writing give me the opportunity to share both loving memories and new ideas with many people. If my prayers are answered—and most of them are—you will pass on some of the love I've shared with you to someone you love.

May the God I love bless you, your kitchen, your meals, and all the people who pass through your life.

Love,

Curtis

P. S. Reading is loving. Please help someone find love through reading. There is a literacy group in your town that needs you as a tutor, or to answer phones, or to provide numerous kinds of assistance. Please volunteer. The millions of nonreading adults need you.

Index